F. Scott Fitzgerald at Work

F. Scott Fitzgerald at Work

The Making of "The Great Gatsby"

Horst H. Kruse

THE UNIVERSITY OF ALABAMA PRESS

Tuscaloosa

The University of Alabama Press
Tuscaloosa, Alabama 35487-0380
uapress.ua.edu

Typeface: Perpetua, Futura and Bodoni

Manufactured in the United States of America
Cover photograph: *The Great Gatsby,* Last Page of the Manuscript. Reproduced from
"The Great Gatsby": A Facsimile of the Manuscript, p. 259; courtesy of Princeton University Library and the Fitzgerald Literary Trust.
Author photograph: Courtesy of Uli Kiefner
Cover design: Mary Elizabeth Watson

∞

The paper on which this book is printed meets the minimum requirements of American National Standard for Information Sciences—Permanence of Paper for Printed Library Materials, ANSI Z39.48-1984.

Library of Congress Cataloging-in-Publication Data

Kruse, Horst Hermann, author.
　F. Scott Fitzgerald at work : the making of "The Great Gatsby" / Horst H. Kruse.
　　pages cm
　Includes bibliographical references and index.
　ISBN 978-0-8173-1839-0 (cloth : alk. paper) — ISBN 978-0-8173-8770-9 (e book)
　1. Fitzgerald, F. Scott (Francis Scott), 1896-1940. Great Gatsby. 2. Fiction—Authorship—Psychological aspects. I. Title.
　PS3511.I9G849　2014
　813'.52—dc23
                                                                    2014006771

Contents

Illustrations

Acknowledgments

My work on *The Great Gatsby* and its sources of inspiration has extended over several decades. In the course of it I have incurred many obligations to individuals and institutions. First and foremost, I owe thanks and gratitude to my wife, Ursula Kruse, as well as to my friend the late Matthew J. Bruccoli. Both have advised, challenged, and encouraged me in my research. Drafts and early versions of the present monograph were read by Ruth Prigozy, Milton R. Stern, Jackson R. Bryer, and Marvin Spevack. As much as from their reading I have profited from extended correspondence with Dan Hardy, Steven Goldleaf, and Natalie A. Naylor, as well as exchanges with Barbara Probst Solomon, Howard G. Comen, and Daniel Strohl.

Whenever possible I have acknowledged in my text or notes the assistance received from individuals. Although many librarians, archivists, and archival volunteers remain anonymous, my thanks go out to them and to the institutions they serve: The National Archives and Records Administration in Washington, DC, in College Park, Maryland, in New York City, New York, and in Pittsfield, Massachusetts (special services were rendered by Mitchell Yockelson, Edward Barnes, and Connie Beach); Cornell University Library and its Division of Reference Services; Princeton University Library; the University of Delaware Library; the University of South Carolina Libraries and the Matthew J. and Arlyn Bruccoli Collection of F. Scott Fitzgerald; the Long Island Studies Institute at Hofstra University; Universitätsbibliothek Köln; the New York Public Library; the Library of Congress; Geheimes Staatsarchiv Preussischer Kulturbesitz Berlin; Landesarchiv Berlin; Staatsarchiv Hamburg; and the Kaliningrad Cathedral Museum. Online access to archival material turned out to provide a special impetus. I am grateful to have been able to avail myself of the services of the Ellis Island Foundation as well as of Ancestry.com, Genealogy.com, and Footnote.com as commercial enterprises.

Generations of my students have explored Fitzgerald with me and enriched my appreciation of his writings. I owe them thanks and gratitude for sharing my interest. And I also thank the international community of Fitzgerald scholars as organized in the F. Scott Fitzgerald Society for providing such a lively forum for the discussion of a work in progress.

I was particularly fortunate, as I was bringing my project to a conclusion, to find in Kirk Curnutt and James W. L. West III the most competent of readers. In their devotion to both the study of Fitzgerald and the development of Fitzgerald studies, these distinguished scholars gave valuable advice.

The University of Alabama Press is a congenial haven for Fitzgerald studies and scholars. Curtis Clark, director; Dan Waterman, acquisitions editor; Vanessa Rusch, managing editor; and Rick Cook, production manager, deserve credit and thanks for their solicitude and care on behalf of this book. Special thanks go to designer Mary Elizabeth Watson for the final cover treatment and to Princeton University Library (Don Skemer) and the Fitzgerald Literary Trust (Craig Tenney, Harold Ober Associates) for use of the cover image.

Permission to use copyrighted material has kindly been granted as follows: (1) by Rosemary Colt (for the estate of Arthur Mizener) to quote from documents in the Arthur Mizener Papers on F. Scott Fitzgerald in the Manuscripts Division, Department of Rare Books and Special Collections, Princeton University Library, as well as the Arthur Mizener Papers in the Special Collections, University of Delaware Library, Newark, Delaware; (2) by Farrar, Straus and Giroux to quote from letters by Edmund Wilson in the Arthur Mizener Papers in the Special Collections, University of Delaware Library. Permission to publish the above materials has also been granted by these two libraries as holders of the documents.

Princeton University Library has further granted permission to quote from one of its letters of Belle Trenholm and one of its letters of Max von

Gerlach in the Arthur Mizener Papers, as well as its clipping "Scott Fitzgerald Lays Success to Reading" in the F. Scott Fitzgerald Papers. Cornell University Library has granted permission to quote from a letter by Mary Harriman Rumsey in the Willard Dickerman Straight Papers, Division of Rare and Manuscript Collections, Kroch Library. Permission to publish Max von Gerlach's letter to Arthur Mizener, c. 1953–54 (page 16), and Max von Gerlach's calling card (page 39) from the Arthur Mizener Papers on F. Scott Fitzgerald has been granted by Princeton University Library; permission to publish a reproduction of Friedrich Lahrs' 1936 drawing "Aussicht von Kant's Fenster [A View From Kant's Window]" (page 104) has been granted by the Kaliningrad Cathedral Museum and Dr. Wolfgang Blumers for the estate of Friedrich Lahrs.

Chapter 3, "*The Great Gatsby:* A View from Kant's Window—Transatlantic Crosscurrents," and brief sections of Chapter 1 appeared previously in *The F. Scott Fitzgerald Review* in 2002 and 2003. I thank the editors for their permission to reprint the material here.

F. Scott Fitzgerald at Work

Introduction

"*The Great Gatsby* is inexhaustible," Matthew J. Bruccoli wrote in his introduction to *New Essays on "The Great Gatsby"* in 1985. A quarter of a century's further work on the novel has not proved him wrong. Surprisingly, Bruccoli's statement also holds for studies of the author's sources and the actual process of the novel's composition. Even as the times recede in which the manuscript was written and revised, and even as the materials the author made use of disappear from view, new facts about the genesis of the novel can be brought to light. And rather than merely adding to our knowledge, they actually correct previous assumptions and change our perspective on *The Great Gatsby* as much as they enhance our assessment and understanding of Fitzgerald's creative imagination.

The four essays in this collection are all concerned with material that Fitzgerald either worked with or worked from. They are the result of journeys of discovery, in a literal sense of the term as much as in a metaphorical sense. While each essay was begun as a separate study and involved its separate journey, and while each was allowed to determine its own development and its own scope—altogether independent of any overarching thesis to prejudice both procedure and findings—they yet converge in their overall conclusions. They all go to confirm my view that the author's flights of fancy, even at their most spectacular, are securely grounded in biographical experience as well as in the social and literary circumstances of his time. The essays thus become chapters in a study of Fitzgerald's working habits at a point in his development as a writer when he was turning away from the largely autobiographical matter of his first two novels and began searching for new materials and a more objective approach in the writing of what became *The Great Gatsby*.

Four such essays, even as they combine to become chapters in a book, do not make an exhaustive study of the writing of Fitzgerald's masterpiece, to be sure. Rather, like all scholarship, they invite and hope to promote further work along the same or similar lines. Still, the essays assembled here do claim to be representative, not merely through the convergence of their method and their findings, but because they deliberately focus on facets of the novel and its writing that before all others would seem to commend themselves to the attention of readers as well as critics and scholars. These facets, in the order of their subsequent arrangement, are the following: the material that provided Fitzgerald with the basic inspiration for his protagonist as much as for his theme and narrative technique, the laying out of the opening chapter of the novel, the inspiration for a pivotal scene in the very center of the work, and the ideological frame for the working out of the final scene in the final chapter of his book.

Reconstructing the biography of Max von Gerlach (in the first essay) as that of a German immigrant with a past as shady as Jay Gatsby's is made out to be in the novel took me on not a few journeys to various archives and libraries in the United States as well as in Germany. It involved lengthy correspondence with authorities high and low and sent me on seemingly endless Internet searches as ever-new material became available online. Along with an earlier version first published in *The F. Scott Fitzgerald Review,* now superseded in its conclusions, the essay has taken me ever since Arthur Mizener's first mention of Max von Guerlach as a model for Jay Gatsby—as long ago as 1951—to come to a satisfactory conclusion.

Another journey, again undertaken in various installments over a period of years, sent me to Long Island to explore its actual and moral geographies in relation to the Fitzgeralds and their circle of friends and neighbors, as well as its role in the infamous eugenics movement. Taking me to highways (such as the Jericho Turnpike) and byways (such as Hitchcock Lane) and involving interviews with scholars, librarians, and local people, the search (as presented in the second essay) helped me to gather insights into the complexity and allusiveness of Fitzgerald's opening chapter.

The journey of discovery that took me east rather than west (as recounted in the third essay) was not a journey primarily in pursuit of knowledge about either *The Great Gatsby* or its author. But what Fitzgerald scholar would travel to Königsberg without Fitzgerald's reference to Kant in mind? The journey east entailed a journey west to explore the circumstances of Fitzgerald's encounter with Kant on the occasion of the bicentennial of the philosopher's birthday. The evidence—the April 30, 1924, issue of *The New Republic,* located in the Library of Congress—proved difficult to establish, and my hotel bill grew accordingly. But there was little need for Matthew Bruccoli to reassure me when I told him about my search and its success: illuminating discoveries such as these are worth every dollar one has to pay.

The fourth journey of discovery (as recounted in the final essay) was, and is, entirely a journey of the mind. It involves imaginary visits to places such as Rome, the prairies of the American West, and Dover Beach—at moments in time from as far back as 1764, 1832, 1851, and 1860 to the beginning of the twentieth century—to observe people pondering the course of history and to view famous sites whose evocation gives resonance to Fitzgerald's very own version of the archetypal experience of historicity as set in the autumn of 1922 on the beach of Long Island Sound in the closing scene of *The Great Gatsby*.

I have not counted the miles or the hours that have gone into the travels involved in completing my research, but traveling as well as research is its own reward. Having Fitzgerald and *The Great Gatsby* as a guide is the richest bonus there is.

Max von Gerlach, the Man Behind Jay Gatsby

A German Immigrant Story and Its Impact on the Composition of *The Great Gatsby*

"...what better right does a man possess than to invent his own antecedents?"
Nick Carraway assessing Jay Gatsby, F. Scott Fitzgerald, *The Great Gatsby: The Revised and Rewritten Galleys* (1990), p. 161

Introduction

There is all but universal agreement that F. Scott Fitzgerald's *The Great Gatsby* occupies a preeminent place in American literature, in terms of popular appeal and critical acclaim, and that Jay Gatsby, the protagonist, more so than any other character in American fiction, embodies national themes and aspirations. The complex story of the novel's achievement is thus fully deserving of the attention it has been given, its verification worthy of further effort. In its powerful mythical implications and profuse dependence on American materials, both historical and contemporary, *The Great Gatsby* has indeed left much room for speculation about the author's actual sources of inspiration. The large number and wide range of parallels and correspondences that have been proposed, literary and otherwise, and the number of real people that have been suggested as models for its cast of characters—Jay Gatsby in particular—are as much a measure of its universal quality as of the interest that the author and his work continue to command. But at the same time the abundance of such proposals also hints at the failure of scholarship to determine basic elements of the history of the making of the novel and calls for a continuing effort at clarification. Jay Gatsby, above all, in his commanding presence of nearly 90 years' standing, is holding out a challenge to explore his actual roots, intriguing as they are in their persistent obscurity.

It is in response to this challenge that I return to the case of Max Gerlach. Apart from Edward M. Fuller, William F. McGee, and Robert C. Kerr, whose contributions to his characterization are considered minor, Gerlach was the only model for Jay Gatsby expressly identified by name in 1947 by Zelda Fitzgerald, the author's wife, shortly before her death. And in 1951 Gerlach himself spoke up and claimed to be the individual who inspired Fitzgerald's protagonist. Despite all research efforts, however, Gerlach remains elusive as an historical personage, so that the extent and the exact nature of his influence on the inception and the composition of *The Great Gatsby* continue to be a matter of debate. Prompted early by Gerlach's German name and carried on in friendly rivalry with Matthew J. Bruccoli, my own explorations eventually led me to the fortuitous discovery of materials in the National Archives and Records Administration in both Washington, DC, and College Park, Maryland, concerning Gerlach's military career in the US Army during World War I, as well as court records in the US District Court for the Southern District of New York concerning his bootleg activities. Working from these and other documents relating to his life both before and after the war, I was able to trace central motifs of the novel and a long list of specific details to incidents in Gerlach's life and thus substantiate previous speculations concerning his role in the genesis of the book. What had escaped my notice at the time— and what I have discovered only since the publication of my findings in *The F. Scott Fitzgerald Review* in 2002—is an essential fact that turns out to hold a key to both Gerlach's personality and its appeal to the author of *The Great Gatsby*—that the circumstances of his life in combination with those of the times he lived in had suggested to Gerlach that he proceed to construct and reconstruct varying accounts of his biography in the interest of his own advancement. His very success in this endeavor of necessity entailed the likelihood of error for those engaged in the study of his activities. This turned my own research into an uncommonly challenging, at times frustrating, but also thoroughly rewarding longtime scholarly adventure on two sides of the Atlantic, an adventure not without its share of pleasant surprises. When proof continued to refuse to emerge to support the widely held view of Gerlach as a wealthy Long Island bootlegger, for instance, the search for further details of his life happened to take me to libraries and archives in Germany rather than in the United States, affording me the advantage of ready access to files partly obscured by linguistic usages and idiosyncrasies in print and handwriting, such as occur in historical documents. These German files, along with a variety of materials freshly available on the Internet, turn out to provide significant additions to earlier information about Max Gerlach and suggest a new configuration of the evidence.

Among the more important facts and documents that have come to light in my renewed search are the following:

- Gerlach was born in Germany rather than in the United States, as he had claimed.
- He came to America at age nine as a half-orphan, the stepson of a German immigrant.
- He used his stepfather's last name, Stork, for nearly two decades.
- He presented various contradictory versions of his life story.
- He temporarily returned to Germany and consequently was entangled with American legal authorities.
- A 1915 photo of Max Stork in New York City Police Department evidence files.
- Additional street addresses and business connections in New York City as well as Chicago and Joliet, Illinois.
- His 1919 visa application with passport photo and personal data.
- Several documents relating to his life after contact with the Fitzgeralds.

All in all, the newly recovered details add up to consolidate the typification of Gerlach's experiences as those of an immigrant and to provide a fabric that would allow Fitzgerald to dramatize these experiences as a prototypical account of the rags-to-riches American success story and—in topical variation—its failure in the growing materialism of the American twenties.

They do not, however, confirm either his role as a big-time bootlegger or as a neighbor of the Fitzgeralds on Long Island. Rather, and more importantly, it emerges that Max Gerlach brought to the novel an intriguingly complex biography in which unusual personal as well as national predicaments combined to shape his abiding quest for identity as an American citizen. And it appears that it was this quest, rather than the bootlegger's lifestyle and wealth, that appealed to Fitzgerald and made him take Gerlach for a model and Gerlach's very quest as his theme. In addition to correcting long-held assumptions about Gerlach and proposing some adjustments in chronology, the present study thus finds its ultimate rationale in having us perceive an altogether different focus in Fitzgerald's interest in his source of inspiration and at the same time giving us a different perspective on the novel.

In some instances, Gerlach's experiences will be shown to reflect Fitzgerald's own encounters, as well as his anxieties and ambitions. And while this may have been one of the reasons Fitzgerald took an interest in Gerlach as a model, such convergences must have made it easy for the author to instill aspects of his own life into that of the fictional character and finally to have them prevail when in the course of writing he began to discover Gerlach's deficiency as a model. As Fitzgerald informed Charles T. Scott in a 1927 inscription in a copy of *The Great Gatsby*, "Gatsby was never quite real to me. His original served for a good enough exterior until about the middle of the book he grew thin and I began to fill him with my own emotional life" (qtd. in *GG Documentary Vol.* 27), echoing an earlier remark in a letter to his friend John Peale Bishop, which stated that Gatsby "started as one man I knew and then changed into myself" (*Letters* 358).

Both statements have given Fitzgerald biographers and scholars a pretext to downplay the importance of Gerlach in the inception of *The Great Gatsby*. But in reality it was a matter of these researchers simply failing to turn up even a minimum of reliable information to begin to appraise Gerlach's true role. In order to assess Fitzgerald's aims and intentions in writing his novel, however, as well as to study the workings of his creative imagination in the process, we are not so much interested in the author's own emotional life that helped to fill in what appeared to him a good enough exterior as we are in the original source of inspiration, the one man who sparked the central idea in all its brilliance and originality. It is this one man, Max Gerlach, and his actual role in the inception of *The Great Gatsby* that will form the primary focus of this investigation.

The Myth of Max von Gerlach, the Long Island Bootlegger

From his first mention in Fitzgerald biography and scholarship, Max Gerlach is referred to as "a Long Island bootlegger" (Mizener, *The Far Side of Paradise* 171) and a "neighbor" of the Fitzgeralds' while they were living at 6 Gateway Drive in Great Neck (Zelda Fitzgerald to Henry Dan Piper as reported by Bruccoli in 1975; *GG Documentary Volume* 20). When documentary evidence failed to emerge to substantiate these facts, the adjective "mysterious" began to attach itself to his name. So persistent and pervasive was this image of Gerlach as a Long Island resident—and so apparently authoritative its presentation in early Fitzgerald biography—that later scholars, myself included, felt inclined to adjust their accounts to fit this supposition. As details of Gerlach's career began to emerge from the newly discovered sources in my earlier search—his employment as a marine gas engineer, machinist, automotive mechanic, and broker of automobiles, along with his knowledge of Spanish, his repeated visits to Cuba, and two convictions on charges of violation of the Volstead Act—they almost naturally prompted my speculations about his activities as a gentleman bootlegger in order to account for his supposed wealth and its attributes during the twenties. But my continued searches—of real estate maps, community directories, telephone books, census records, and other material—have failed to yield the slightest trace of a Max Gerlach living in either Great Neck or in any of the adjoining Long Island towns—reason enough to reexamine the early accounts that would seem to place him and his impressive mansion in that neighborhood.

Zelda's identification of Gerlach occurred in an interview conducted in 1947 by Fitzgerald scholar Henry Dan Piper, whose conjectural transcription of the name resulted in the faulty spelling "Guerlach." The information he received from Zelda was about "a neighbor named von Guerlach or something who was said to be General Pershing's nephew and was in trouble over bootlegging," as Piper put it in 1974 in his answer to a query from Matthew J.

Bruccoli (*GG Documentary Volume* 20). As early as 1950, Piper had also passed on the information to Arthur Mizener, Fitzgerald's first biographer. In his own 1965 study of the author, *F. Scott Fitzgerald: A Critical Portrait*, as well as in other published work, Piper made no reference to Gerlach whatsoever. Piper's widow, Roberta—for her part insisting that the inspiration for Gatsby "came from Fitzgerald's imagination" and that, therefore, the quest for the prototype of Gatsby must remain "a fruitless search" (letter to *Princeton Alumni Weekly*, November 14, 2002)—concluded that Piper had quite deliberately disposed of "Gurlach" and whatever information he had received about him from Zelda, that he "probably didn't consider it of any great importance" ("The Ghost in My House" 3). But Piper quite obviously did believe in the essential usefulness of establishing and discussing Fitzgerald's sources, as evidenced by his meticulous account of the activities of Edward M. Fuller (*FSF: A Critical Portrait* 115–20). It is through Piper's painstaking reconstruction of Fuller's personality and commercial transactions that this Long Island businessman now figures as a significant contributory source in the creation of Gatsby. Piper's failure to pursue the case of Gerlach was hardly a deliberate dismissal of him as a potential prototype. It was rather that, quite unlike Fuller, Gerlach had not left a conspicuous trail of evidence of his existence in contemporary newspapers, from which Piper sought most of his information. Piper, therefore, was clearly unable to turn up any material about Gerlach to help him assess and appreciate the latter's role in the compositional process of Fitzgerald's novel. And failing to do so, he never came to see any reason to correct his idiosyncratic faulty spelling of "Guerlach," continuing to use it, in fact, as late as 1974 in his reply to Bruccoli's query.

The first published mention of Max Gerlach as a model for Gatsby occurred in a somewhat ambiguous add-on footnote in Arthur Mizener's *The Far Side of Paradise* in 1951. As Mizener drafted his chapter on *The Great Gatsby*—late in 1947 or early in 1948—he started out with information received from critic Edmund Wilson, Fitzgerald's friend and fellow Princetonian, with whom Mizener had been consulting since the early 1940s about his projected biography. The critic had in effect steered Mizener to Wilson's own play, *The Crime in the Whistler Room* of 1924, and Mizener proceeded to quote the following scene in which the protagonist, a young novelist named Simon, describes his encounter with a wealthy bootlegger:

He's a gentleman bootlegger: his name is Max Fleischman. He lives like a millionaire. Gosh, I haven't seen so much to drink since Prohibition. . . . Well, Fleischman was making a damn ass of himself bragging about how much his tapestries were worth and how much his bathroom was worth and how he never wore a shirt twice—and he had a revolver studded with diamonds. . . . And he finally got on my nerves—I was a little bit stewed—and I told him I wasn't impressed by his ermine-lined revolver: I told him he was nothing but a bootlegger, no matter how much money he made. . . . I told him I never would have come into his damn house if it hadn't been to be polite and that it was a torture to stay in a place where everything was in such terrible taste. (*The Far Side of Paradise* 171–72)

Mizener took notes of what Wilson said (see Mizener's April 12, 1948, letter), and, writing to him in March 1948, reminded Wilson to have claimed that "Simon's description of Max Fleischman [. . .] was really Fitzgerald's description of an evening with the bootlegger who gave him the idea for Gatsby's grandeur" and also that Wilson had "repeated the description fairly literally" (see Mizener's March 22, 1948, letter). And Wilson, although clearly rejecting the prevalent identification of the young novelist in his play as his friend Fitzgerald[1] (except for "certain traits suggested by him"), had written back to confirm that "the incident about the bootlegger was [. . .] true of Scott, as I told you" (see Mizener's March 30, 1948, letter). This was reason enough for Mizener to conclude that the Long Island bootlegger described in *The Crime in the Whistler Room* was the actual model for Jay Gatsby, if only in the externals of his existence. Moreover, there was a curious piece of evidence that appeared to corroborate his conclusion. None other than Fitzgerald himself had glossed the same passage in his copy of a reprint of the play (in Wilson's collection entitled *This Room and This Gin and These Sandwiches*) in a marginal note on page 75, which read, "I had told Bunnny my plan for Gatsby" (*FSF: Inscriptions*, item 86). As will emerge, however, Mizener was wrong in his conclusion. Fitzgerald's comment certainly need not be read to vouch for the incident as literal transcription of factual experience. And the wording chosen by Wilson, while referring to a bootlegger, does not actually suggest that this bootlegger was Fitzgerald's model for Jay Gatsby but, rather, simply someone "who gave him the idea for Gatsby's grandeur" (as Mizener himself had put it).

As to the latter point, the name Max Fleischman as it occurs in Wilson's play probably is not a fictional substitution for a real name at all. In the summer of 1923 Zelda was telling the Kalmans, her St. Paul friends, that since their arrival in Great Neck she had "unearthed some of the choicest bootleggers" (including Fleischman) (qtd. in Bruccoli, *Some Sort of Epic Grandeur* 184). At the time specified there actually were two people named Fleischmann: Brothers Julius and Max, immensely wealthy yeast producers variously involved in much-publicized charges of manufacturing illegal alcohol and owners of residences on Long Island.[2] Julius held an estate on Sands Point Road (now Middle Neck Road); Max had built The Lindens, an impressive mansion in Sands Point Village at the northern tip of Manhasset Neck, the actual East Egg of *The Great Gatsby*.[3] And it appears that as an author Wilson had practically no qualms about using the names and portraits of real people in his play. In addition to Max Fleischmann, for instance, in lines deleted by Mizener from the passage in his biography, there is "Madge Fox, the movie actress, [. . .] she's a mess: she's got pink hair," as well as "the man who produces the wisecracks for the Merry-Go-Round Revue" (75). The former was a notorious vaudeville actress popularly known at the time as the Flip Flop Girl, whereas the latter can be easily identified as Gene Buck, musical comedy producer Florenz Ziegfeld's lyricist and right hand, a prominent Manhasset resident and "one of Fitzgerald and Lardner's inebriated friends" (Goldstein 36). Although the passage from *The Crime in the Whistler Room* (along with the details deleted in Mizener's quotation of it) does point to *The Great Gatsby*, it does not appear to take us back to the person of Max Gerlach as the actual source of its protagonist. What Wilson renders in his play is more likely to reflect and to document an advanced stage in the unfolding of what Fitzgerald explicitly refers to as his "plan for Gatsby" rather than to represent a faithful description of a personal adventure that the author himself may have had. And such a *plan* could well have grown out of visits that Fitzgerald paid to a number of Long Island mansions, including those of Fleischmann and other bootleggers, as well as to residents specifically named by him in his

Ledger and in a list of sources for *The Great Gatsby* compiled at a later date (in a copy of André Malraux's *Man's Hope* of 1938).[4] It is interesting, too, that as early as the second installment of his "Imaginary Conversations" published in *The New Republic,* April 30, 1924, Wilson had had the progressive Fitzgerald tell the conservative Van Wyck Brooks about his unbounded admiration for the lifestyles of the very rich, of "the Goulds and the Hills and the Harrimans": "Think of being able to buy anything you wanted—houses, railroads, enormous industries!—food, drinks, automobiles, stunning clothes for your wife—clothes like nobody else in the world could wear—all the greatest paintings in Europe, all the books that had ever been written, in magnificent bindings! Think of being able to give a stupendous house party that would go on for days and days, with everything that anybody could want to drink and a medical staff in attendance and the biggest jazz orchestra in the city alternating day and night!" (254). While it is true that these are remarks that are merely ascribed to Fitzgerald, they are in fact close enough to what is known of his predilections and interests to suggest that the quoted details that figure in the "creative exhilaration" of the wealthy had actually been a matter of discourse between the two friends. Most of these details recur in *The Great Gatsby* as well. Along with the episode incorporated in *The Crime in the Whistler Room,* they indicate that Fitzgerald had indeed been engaged in telling Wilson about his "plan for Gatsby," a plan possibly with several options as yet, while Wilson, as a writer, had begun to pay attention to Fitzgerald in his fiction as well as in his critical work—both indicative of the close rapport that existed between the men. Although Mizener apparently did not delve deeply into the matter of Fleischman's identity, he is probably right in asserting that Fitzgerald knew the real Fleischmann "only slightly" and that, moreover, the known details "account only for the externals of Gatsby" (172). But this assertion would be true only as long as the reference is solely to the actual Max Fleischmann (or to the actual person who figures as Max Fleischman in Wilson's play) and ceases to be true once Mizener added his footnote to suggest that this same person "was a Teutonic-featured man named von Guerlach" (336 n9). This footnote—actually the extension of an existing footnote for the quotation from *The Crime in the Whistler Room,* and apparently made at a point when the information could no longer be accommodated in the body of the text—was the result of his learning of Zelda's remarks about Gerlach from Piper "as a sort of casual, amusing throwaway line in a conversation over drinks at the MLA meeting in New York in 1950," as Roberta Piper disparagingly recounts in 2006 ("The Ghost in My House" 3). Like Henry Dan Piper, Mizener at that point had no independent information about Gerlach, but Zelda's identification of him as "a neighbor" who was "in trouble over bootlegging"—perhaps along with the fact that Fleischman and von Guerlach are German names—obviously led him to conclude that Fleischman and von Guerlach were actually one and the same person. And this, by implication, induced him to transfer his observations on Fleischman (as a "Long Island bootlegger whom Fitzgerald knew only slightly" [172]) to von Gerlach as the actual model identified by Zelda. This happened about a year after Wilson had completed his reading of Mizener's manuscript (cf. his letter to Mizener on February 22, 1950, 1) and when their exchange of information and correspondence about biographical details had all but ended. And so the chance was lost that, as a potential witness, Wilson might have corrected or specified Mizener's account of Fitzgerald's encounter with the prototype of Gatsby. The chance was also lost that Wilson point out that what he had maintained about the actual experience behind the encounter between Simon and Max Fleischman as described in *The Crime in the Whistler Room* was that it had given Fitzgerald the idea not so much for Gatsby as a character or a protagonist, but, rather and solely, for Gatsby's grandeur (as Mizener had in fact repeated Wilson's argument when he wrote to him on March 22, 1948).

It is hard to tell if it was lack of genuine interest in the question of who inspired the character of Jay Gatsby or indeed the lack of specific information about possible models that caused Mizener to downplay the value of source materials in general and to conclude, with reference to Fleischman as he emerges in the scene quoted from Wilson's play, that "these details account only for the externals of Gatsby." And such externals, as he pointed out, were of little importance: "the vulgar and romantic young man Fitzgerald found somewhere *inside himself* to fill this outline of a character is what matters" (172; emphasis added). This statement typifies Mizener's approach throughout his biography, and is a measure of the importance to him of fusing Gatsby and Fitzgerald, as well as to mutually explaining the author and his protagonist, that he neglected to pursue the chance of a meeting with the actual Max Gerlach when the opportunity arose in 1951 and again in 1954. The incident bears recounting for what can be learned from it not only about Fitzgerald's model but also about Fitzgerald's biographer and the latter's procedure of "mutually corroborating art and life," as novelist Richard Ford has aptly called it (582).

In the years prior to the publication of *The Far Side of Paradise*, Mizener had begun to use the radio as well as journals and magazines such as *The Atlantic Monthly, Partisan Review, The Kenyon Review*, and *Life* to draw attention to Fitzgerald as well as to his own forthcoming study. When, probably early in 1951, he had appeared on Mary Margaret McBride's popular radio show in New York City, a secretary informed him immediately afterward, "Mr. Mizener, there is a man on the telephone to speak to you who says he is Jay Gatsby."[5] This man was none other than Max Gerlach, whose readiness to identify himself to the author's biographer and whose outright claim to actually *be* Jay Gatsby (a claim that has gone virtually unknown, even among Fitzgerald scholars, to this very day) are integral to perhaps the strongest case to be made for him as the principal source of Fitzgerald's protagonist. Mizener did not talk to Gerlach at the time and somehow never managed to provide an opportunity for Gerlach to present his story. In fact, there is reason to assume that, having worked out and published his own account of the writing of *The Great Gatsby*, Mizener was none too eager to invite divergent evidence. Writing to Gerlach from Carleton College in Northfield, Minnesota, on January 15, 1951, and still addressing him as "von Guerlach," Mizener explained the information he had about him (and in doing so implicitly confirmed that he indeed considered Wilson's "Fleischman" and Piper's "von Guerlach" to be one and the same person, the former name having served Wilson as a substitute for the latter as he came to write his play): "What I knew was this—Edmund Wilson, the literary critic, told me that Fitzgerald came to his house, apparently from yours, and told him with great fascination about the life you were leading. Naturally, it fascinated him as all splendor did but Wilson couldn't remember your name" (AM to MvG, TS copy). In view of the texts of *The Crime in the Whistler Room* and *The Great Gatsby*, there is reason to believe that Mizener glossed over what he believed had actually been said in order to flatter Gerlach and elicit a reply. But in what follows in his letter he clearly indicated to Gerlach the kind of a reply he preferred to receive: "I feel reasonably sure from what Fitzgerald did with other real people in his work that Gatsby is not very like you, but I would be interested to know from you, if you will tell me, what parts of the character seemed to you real and what invented. I would guess Fitzgerald used your appearance to some extent, something perhaps pretty close to your home and something, though not all, from actual parties you gave. I would also guess that Gatsby's character, his motives, and his ideas were not yours." Gerlach himself, rather than refer to this exhaustive but purely speculative assessment of his role as a model in the writing of the novel, informed Mizener that he would like to talk to him personally instead of communicating with him "through other channels": "I would prefer it this way as there are few people to whom I could express my candid comments with regard to F. Scott Fitzgerald, who might not, perhaps, misinterpret them" (Letter to Mizener, July 2, 1951). It must be taken into account that Gerlach, having blinded himself in a failed suicide attempt by pistol in 1939, would have had to call on secretarial help for every communication. Although he went on to tell Mizener that he was "looking forward with pleasure to having a long talk with you and being of any help I can in this fine work you are doing," and although such invitations were repeated until as late as 1954,[6] no occasion ever presented itself for him to explain just what it was that the wording he had chosen was meant to insinuate regarding his relations with the author.

There is good reason to assume, in view of Gerlach's apparent refusal to assent to Mizener's assessment of his role in the composition of *The Great Gatsby* and the "candid comments with regard to F. Scott Fitzgerald" that he was prepared to make, that Gerlach had additional specific information to communicate. Given the circumstances of his life in total blindness and apparent isolation,[7] however, it is unlikely that written records of any kind will ever be found. Whatever Gerlach would have had to communicate will in all probability remain unknown forever. It stands to reason, however, that what Mizener would have learned from Gerlach, from the man who had identified himself as being the "actual" Jay Gatsby, was that he was not someone "whom Fitzgerald knew only slightly," that he was not a person to be characterized as a "Long Island bootlegger," that the details of "Fleischman" that "account [. . .] for the externals of Gatsby" are not also the details of Gerlach, and that Gerlach's details would seem to account (also in the light of my

MURRAY HILL 2-5140

The Mansfield Hotel

TWELVE WEST FORTY-FOURTH STREET

NEW YORK 36, N. Y.

Dear Arthur,
    Just a line acknowledging your last
letter and sending my best regards. I'm hoping
that on your next trip to New York we can have a
pleasant chat about F. Scott, the man and his times.
Trusting that your continental sojourn was interesting
and hoping to hear from you soon....

                            Max von Gerlach

                                    MG/ EM

1. Max von Gerlach, letter to Arthur Mizener, c. 1953–54. Princeton University Library.

previous findings) for much more in Fitzgerald's protagonist than his mere externals. And the sum of what he would have learned from Gerlach would also have given him as well as us a much better perception of what Fitzgerald "found inside himself" to fill in what he had found missing in his model's emotional life. But Mizener, to all appearances, was little touched by Gerlach's attempts to communicate with him. There is no small irony in the fact that two days after Gerlach was buried, Mizener should have remarked, in a letter of November 5, 1958, to the editor of the *Times Literary Supplement,* that *The Great Gatsby* was based on Fitzgerald's experiences in Great Neck and that "the rather remote model for Gatsby himself, a man named Max von Guerlach, is still alive to tell about it."[8] The faulty spelling of Gerlach's name continued to stand unglossed in Mizener's correction copy of *The Far Side of Paradise* (Arthur Mizener Papers , Princeton University Library, Box 5, Folder 1). It remained uncorrected in the 1965 revised edition as well as in all later publications of Mizener's, leaving the (incidental) addition of Gerlach's first name, Max, as the only tangible result of their otherwise abortive interchange. By the time of Mizener's writing of the popular *F. Scott Fitzgerald and His World*, which appeared simultaneously in the United States and in Great Britain in 1972, his view of Gerlach and his role in the composition of *The Great Gatsby* had consolidated, unsupported by any further factual evidence, in the following brief statement: "[Fitzgerald] more or less stumbled on the fashionable Long Island bootlegger, Max Von Guerlach, who gave him his idea for Gatsby" (68). The transference of the externals of "Fleischman" to Gerlach seems complete: the "neighbor" of Zelda's report, a "Teutonic-featured man named von Guerlach" who was "in trouble over bootlegging," had finally become "the fashionable Long Island bootlegger, Max Von Guerlach." Given the impact of Mizener's work on future Fitzgerald studies, it is understandable why much of the subsequent search to resolve the mysteries surrounding the elusive Max von Gerlach should have been conducted along the wrong lines and why the assessment of his true role in the compositional process of *The Great Gatsby* should thus have been impaired.

It was not until 1975 that Matthew Bruccoli announced the discovery (in Fitzgerald's scrapbook at the Princeton University Library) of a note dated July 20, 1923, to Fitzgerald from a man named Gerlach that additional factual evidence came to light to strengthen the link between Jay Gatsby and Gerlach and to correct the faulty spelling of the latter's name ("'How Are You and the Family Old Sport'—Gerlach and Gatsby"). The note (on an unidentified 1923 newspaper photo of the Fitzgeralds) read: "Enroute from the coast— Here for a few days on business—How are you and the family old sport?," thus using what has since been called Gatsby's "defining expression" (Bruccoli, "Explanatory Notes," *GG* 189) over the signature of "Gerlach." While Bruccoli's brief article does correct Piper's conjectural spelling and advance recognition of Gerlach's importance for the portrait of Gatsby, it still perpetuates the view of him as "a Long Island bootlegger" more or less identical with the "gentleman bootlegger named Max Fleischman" whom Fitzgerald supposedly had described to Wilson. Continuing along these lines, the article also reproduces a photo from the *New York Evening Post* of January 18, 1930, of "Max Gerlach, wealthy yachtsman," a designation that Bruccoli glosses as "sometimes a euphemism for rumrunner" (*GG Documentary Volume* 20). In addition to observing that Fitzgerald's saving of the clipping and pasting it in his scrapbook indicates he was indeed interested in Gerlach, what has per-

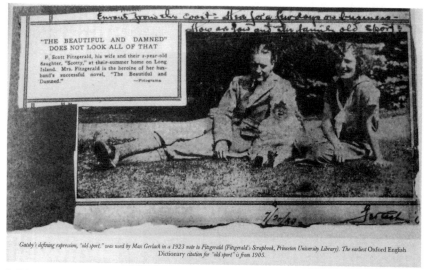

Gatsby's defining expression, "old sport," was used by Max Gerlach in a 1923 note to Fitzgerald (Fitzgerald's Scrapbook, Princeton University Library). The earliest Oxford English Dictionary citation for "old sport" is from 1905.

2. "How are you and the family old sport?" Gerlach's 1923 note to Fitzgerald, reproduced from F. Scott Fitzgerald's "The Great Gatsby": A Documentary Volume, p. 21.

haps not been adequately perceived are two further aspects of the note: First, that the general tone of Gerlach's remarks to Fitzgerald and the salutation "old sport" seem to presuppose a somewhat longer term of acquaintance between the two people, its beginning possibly even antedating the arrival of the Fitzgeralds on Long Island in mid-October 1922. Second, that the note presupposes a somewhat longer period of absence on the part of Gerlach, who does not seem to be living at the time (or is perhaps no longer living) on Long Island at all. These facts further call into question Gerlach's presumed identity as "a fashionable Long Island bootlegger," an identity that nonetheless continues to be taken for granted by most Fitzgerald scholars.[9] The sum of what has been recovered about the life and personality of Max Gerlach would seem to suggest that, although at one point he may have been a neighbor of the Fitzgeralds and "in trouble over bootlegging," as Zelda recalled, he was "a fashionable Long Island bootlegger" merely through Mizener's conflation of him with the character Max Fleischman as portrayed by Edmund Wilson, while what Wilson himself rendered was an episode that draws on some of the various materials that were there to serve Fitzgerald in his endeavor to enhance the figure of Max Gerlach as his primary source of inspiration. It appears that the actual Max Gerlach and Fitzgerald had met under

3. Max von Gerlach, "Wealthy Yachtsman," photographed during a psittacosis scare, *New York Evening Journal*, January 18, 1930. Reproduced from *"The Great Gatsby": A Documentary Volume*, p. 20.

different circumstances than those suggested by Wilson's play and that Gerlach impressed the author, not through his Long Island mansion and spectacular wealth, but rather through other aspects of Gerlach's personality that touched Fitzgerald and then became essential for the genesis of his novel. A survey of basic dates and data concerning Gerlach's life will help to define and to locate such aspects. It will define stages and experiences of his biography as stages and experiences of a typical immigrant story, their unique particularization tending to highlight rather than blur constituent elements and phases of acculturation involved in the process of becoming an American.

The Gerlach Story: Biographical Data vs. His Biography as Perceived by Gerlach

During his lifetime—spanning from pre-World War I to post-World War II—Max Gerlach never was a person to command general interest. His life, therefore, is not a matter of public record. As an immigrant, a German-born citizen, a boy who lost his father early, the stepson of an older man, an applicant for an officer's commission in the US Army, a man in trouble over bootlegging, a dynamic businessman, a suicide survivor, and a blind man for nearly two decades, Gerlach faced many challenges to present amenable versions of the circumstances of his life and those of his family. While these varying accounts and the motivations for their telling will be found to hold a key to the personality of Max Gerlach as well as to the appeal he held for Fitzgerald as a model for his protagonist, they also result in unreliable information about the basic facts of Gerlach's biography. The problem of obtaining accurate data is exacerbated by the imperfect state of relevant documentation, due to spelling and computing errors, faulty transcriptions, misfiled records, and plain inaccessibility of documents, in addition to arbitrary governmental and administrative restrictions. The following details of Max Gerlach's biography emerge as facts ascertainable beyond all reasonable doubt.

Max Gerlach was born on October 12, 1885, in Germany. While the exact place of birth and his birth certificate have not been found, it is certain that for a time his family lived in or around Berlin, the nation's capital, while he was an infant. Gerlach variously stated that his father's name was Ferdinand Gerlach, that he held a position under Emperor Friedrich III as well as served as a lieutenant in the German Army, and that he died as early as 1887. Records of the German Royal Court in Berlin indicate that a Ferdinand Gerlach worked from 1874 to 1877 as Geheimer Kanzlei-Sekretär in the Ministry of the Royal House of Hohenzollern in Berlin, an employment that answers to Gerlach's description of his father as "having filled the position of secretary, or held some other post under Fredrich III, the present German Emperor's father," as quoted in a report prepared by the American Protective League in 1918 (Brennan 2). As to Ferdinand Gerlach's military service, the comprehensive annual records of the Royal Prussian Army contain entries for a Second Lieutenant named Gerlach (first names not being included in any of these entries) who served as Reserve Officer in the Sixth Pomeranian Infantry Regiment No. 49 from 1883 onward. The 1889 volume contains an entry noting the death of said Lieutenant Gerlach, which means that he died in 1888 or possibly at the end of 1887 (*Rang- und Quartier-Liste ... 1889* 450), confirming the information given by Max Gerlach about his father's death. It also indicates that Max Gerlach was born the son of a commoner rather than a nobleman, as he later claimed, and that his father was not Jewish, since Jews were not allowed to become Reserve Officers in the Prussian Army at that time.

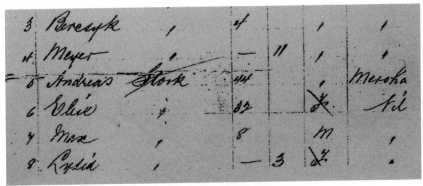

4. Detail from ship manifest of *SS Furnessia,* documenting Max Gerlach's arrival in New York City on November 30, 1894, as a member of the Stork family. Ellis Island Foundation.

About four years later, in 1892, Max's mother, Elizabeth Gerlach—born in December 1863 and also mother to an elder son named Bruno (born in November 1884)—married Andreas Stork, a merchant. A daughter, Lydia, was born early in 1894, and in November of that same year the couple and two children, Max and Lydia (along with Max Muller, a "hatter," age 33, who may have been Elizabeth's brother), emigrated to the United States via Glasgow, Scotland. All were mistakenly listed as Danish nationals on the passenger manifest, perhaps because they may have traveled from the continent via an Esbjerg feeder line (all information taken from Ship Manifest of *SS Furnessia*). They took up residence at 144 Herriot Street in Yonkers, New York, where Andreas (having his name anglicized to Andrew) worked as a hatmaker, probably in the Yonkers Waring Hat Company. By 1900, Lydia had died,[10] and in 1902 Andrew passed away. *Turner's Directory of Yonkers* for 1903 lists Elizabeth Stork as the widow of Andrew, with Max Stork, a messenger (as in the 1902 directory [549]), living at the same address (582). The 1904 directory lists Max as an engineer, still living with his mother at the above address (597). He continued living with the family even when his mother married a third time in 1905 or 1906. Her new husband, Thomas J. Reilly, an English-born Irishman, was 20 years younger, making him just two years older than Max. They all moved to Chicago for a time,[11] but the 1910 Federal Census shows them back in New York City, living at 1394 Second Avenue. The census also lists Max as having been married for two years, but his wife's name does not

5. Max Stork (Max Gerlach), 1915. Photo in New York City police department files. New York City Municipal Archives online gallery, police department evidence: pde_0368.

appear as a member of the household, and the marriage ended in divorce around 1912. *Trow's General Directory* for 1910 additionally lists Max A. Stork as a merchant, with a business at 99 2nd Avenue (1445).

Though still living in his mother's household, Max had long since begun an independent life and a career of his own. When he arrived in the United States at age 9, he had probably had four years of regular schooling in Germany. In the new country he started five years of what he himself termed "private tuition & studies in every branch of Automobile mechanics, practical and technically" (Ordnance Department Personalia Sheet). In 1900, at age 15, he went to Mexico as a machinist on a motor boat, and after his return to the United States in 1903 (Ship Manifest *SS Vigilancia*)—irrespective of having himself listed as messenger in the Yonkers directories of 1902 and 1903—began a long and varied career working in the automotive field, in the United States as well as Cuba, as a garage mechanic and manager, a promoter of auto racing, a car salesman, and a car dealer.[12] It may have been his business activity that occasioned trips to Europe; US passenger lists record his arrival on January 4, 1911, in New York City from Southampton, and in 1913 to 1914 he spent some time in Germany, returning to Boston via London and Liverpool on October 10, 1914. Considering his work in Yonkers as well as in Havana (Cuba), New York City, and possibly Chicago and Joliet (Illinois),[13] one can say that he actually grew up with—and knew how to take advantage of—the phenomenal growth of the automobile industry in the United States. So when in 1918 Max Gerlach (who had begun to resume his birth name but also continued to be known as Stork throughout the decade and even somewhat unaccountably appears as Max Stork in 1915 New York City Police Department evidence that provides us with a photo documenting his appearance at age 29[14]) applied for a major's commission in the Ordnance Department of the US Army to serve at the Raritan Arsenal's Motor Instruction School, he was singularly qualified for that post. Gerlach served from August 15, 1918, as a First Lieutenant at the Raritan Arsenal in Metuchen, New Jersey, and at the port of embarkation, Hoboken, New Jersey, managing the logistics and teaching the handling of automotive equipment that turned out to lend the American Expeditionary Force its particular fighting strength.

On March 29, 1919, he was appointed to the Board of Officers of the Headquarters at the Raritan Arsenal. About a year after the armistice of November 11, 1918, Gerlach received his honorable discharge, effective October 31, 1919 (Gerlach, Index Card). Immediately afterward he applied for a US passport to travel to Havana, Cuba, for a vacation, sailing in December 1919 and returning on March 9, 1920, aboard the *SS Morro Castle* (Ship Manifest of *SS Morro Castle*). The US address he gave was that of the Raritan Arsenal, even though he may have returned to the household of his mother and Thomas Reilly (her third husband), who had also moved to Metuchen, where Thomas's younger brother had taken up work at the arsenal (1920 United States Federal Census). No trace of Max Gerlach is to be found in 1921, but in 1922 the New York City Telephone Directories of May and October list him as living at 178 Fifth Avenue in an apartment house across from the Flatiron Building (*New York City Telephone Directory, May 10, 1922*, 309; *October 11, 1922*, 319. The entry is for Gerlach, M[ax] S[tork]). The next piece of evidence is his July 20, 1923, note to Fitzgerald, which shows him to be "en route from the coast" (i.e., California) on a business trip to the East. On April 7, 1924, Max Gerlach—now married to Elena Gerlach, age 24—is shown to arrive from Cuba in New York City. Of the two addresses listed on the ship's manifest, 42 Broadway obviously is a business address, while 24 East 40th Street, between Fifth and Madison Avenues, could be his private residence (Ship Manifest of *SS Esperanza*). It should be noted at this point that, although there may be gaps in the record of his addresses, there is no indication that at any time between 1920 and 1924 (the period during which he and the Fitzgeralds must have met) Gerlach ever lived on Long Island, let alone in a conspicuous mansion. Nor is there any indication that Gerlach had as yet become a person of particular wealth, his 1922 Fifth Avenue address notwithstanding. No further trace of him is to be found until October 1926, when the New York City Telephone Directory lists his address as 51 West 58th Street, just a few buildings from the Plaza Hotel (453). It is at this address where the following year he was found to have possessed and sold liquor, resulting in two court cases that were heard, on May 9 and August 5, 1927, before the US District Court with jurisdiction over New York City, involving Max V. Gerlach or Max Gerlach on charges of violation of the Volstead Act.[15] After that, there is again no trace of him until June 1929, when he obtained a US passport issued in Washington, DC,[16] and January 1930, when the photo appeared in the *New York Evening Post* showing Max Gerlach the "wealthy yachtsman, kissing a parrot during a psittacosis epidemic." A year later, New York passenger lists document his arrival on May 15, 1931, from Hamburg, Germany, aboard the *SS Hamburg,* his listed US address being given as the prestigious New York Fraternity Club at 22 East 38th Street, New York City (New York Passenger Lists, 1820–1957). The corresponding passenger lists kept in the Staatsarchiv in Hamburg indicate that Gerlach was traveling tourist class and had visited the Free City of Danzig. Although he was ostensibly traveling alone, an American widow named Estelle Rolle (born May 22, 1898) was traveling the same route (Hamburger Passagierlisten 1850–1934, Band 390, Blatt 48; Hamburg Passenger Lists, Handwritten Indexes, 1855–1934, vol. 174). In the summer of 1939 Gerlach came to Flushing and "went into partnership with a man, whose name was not learned, in an open air automobile business" called Park Central Motors, located at 150-10 Northern Boulevard. In November "he and his partner disagreed and decided to close out the firm." As a consequence of his "financial reverses," Gerlach attempted suicide, blinding himself permanently when he shot himself in the

6. Max Stork Gerlach tombstone. Long Island National Cemetery, Farmingdale, New York, 2005. Author photo.

head while in the apartment of a girlfriend at 14 Jones Street in Greenwich Village on December 21, 1939.[17] The 1940 Federal Census (taken as of April 1) lists "Max Gurloch" as one of 36 "inmates" in the State Blind Asylum at 605 First Avenue in New York City. The same institution, now termed the "Blind Man's Club," figures as the address on Max S. Gerlach's Draft Registration Card of April 1942. Records show that on March 26, 1950, Gerlach arrived at Idlewild International Airport on a flight from Havana, Cuba, returning to an address at 232 East 44th Street (Passenger List, Linea Aeropostal Venezolana). New York City Telephone Directories indicate that from 1950 to 1953 he lived at 236 East 34th Street and then moved to the Mansfield Hotel at 12 West 44th Street, where Gerlach lived until 1956. He subsequently moved to his last address at the Van Cortlandt Hotel, 142 West 49th Street, close to Radio City Music Hall. Max Gerlach died on October 18, 1958, at Bellevue Hospital, New York City, and was buried on November 3, 1958, at the US Veterans Gravesite, Section U, Site 375, in the Long Island National Cemetery at Farmingdale, New York, in a pine casket supplied by the US Veterans Administration.[18]

Going by these details, Gerlach's life seems an unlikely story on which an author would be moved to build a novel. As Jonathan Fegley remarks, "Gatsby's historical models, the Long Island bootlegger Max Gerlach and the New York stock swindler Edward M. Fuller, suggest little of the Platonic idealist" (131). This is certainly true of Edward M. Fuller as it is of Fleischmann, Robert C. Kerr, and other real people from whom Fitzgerald borrowed for the composite characterization of his protagonist. But it is not at all true for Gerlach, certainly not in Gerlach's own view of himself. And it was through Gerlach's self-view that Fitzgerald must have come to learn about his story. The drama and literary potential inherent in Gerlach's life emerge from the following series of documents, each reflecting his own presentation and interpretation of biographical data. They all reflect Gerlach's being caught in the dilemma of owing loyalty to two different nations and cultures, as much as they record stages in the difficult process of Americanization in times of war.[19]

Gerlach's Application for an Embassy Passport, Berlin, August 1914

On October 3, 1913, Gerlach, sailing from Montreal, Canada, aboard the SS *Grampian,* arrived in Glasgow to proceed to the Continent for what turned out to be a stay of about ten months. The trip's actual purpose, whether business or private or both, remains unknown. While Gerlach lists his occupation as that of a "salesman," he spent some time at the German seaside resort of Misdroy on the island of Wollin on the Baltic Coast, a place especially popular with vacationers from the German capital. The outbreak of World War I on the first day of August 1914 found Gerlach in Berlin, living at 65 Fasanenstrasse, probably in the Pensionat of Emma Nitzscher (*Berliner Addressbuch*

1914 220). As a German-born male, age 28, he must have seen himself in immediate danger of being drafted into the German Army. It probably was this predicament that prompted him to seek out and prevail upon Major Ryan of the American Embassy to help him obtain an American Embassy passport that would allow him to leave Germany at once and return to the United States. For a young man whose German father had served the Emperor both as a secretary and an officer and who spoke the German language and had returned to the country of his birth for an extended visit, this act now marked a deliberate decision in favor of the United States as his adopted country. It may have been this choice that was within his plight to prove the status of his citizenship without papers and of having merely incomplete information about (or simply memory of) the circumstances of his birth and emigration. The data and facts that Gerlach provided, and which the embassy accepted as adequate to the purpose, constitute an early version of a partially spurious biography invented to resolve his conflict of loyalties as well as to promote his immediate interests. In his Passport Application Form for a "Person Claiming Citizenship Through Naturalization of Husband or Parent" he gave October 12, 1887, as his date of birth and the name of "Norderei" as the place where he was born.

The mistake concerning the year is compensated for by his correct age, but the name of the town he claimed to have been born in, even if allowance is made for a misspelling, does not show up on any map or in any list of communities in Germany.[20] In specifying the data of his immigration, he correctly listed Glasgow as the European port of departure and the *Furnes[s]ia* as the vessel he sailed on, but incorrectly gave February 20, 1889, as his date of arrival in the United States. Similarly incorrect is the year 1890 for naturalization of his mother before the County Court of Yonkers, New York, the fact as such needing to be stated to account for his own (as opposed to his mother's) US citizenship. The form was filled in on August 3, 1914, and the Oath of Allegiance required in connection with the application was administered on August 4, 1914, by Roland B. Harvey, Second Secretary of the Embassy. As a consequence, Gerlach was able to leave Germany on an Embassy passport for London, where he stayed for about three weeks before managing to secure passage from Liverpool to Boston. Even if it is faulty memory that can be blamed for some of the inaccuracies in the application, Gerlach can

7. Max A. Gerlach, 1914 application for Berlin Embassy passport. National Archives and Records Administration II, College Park, Maryland.

be said to have extricated himself from an awkward situation by providing partially incorrect information and thus restyling his own past. And as readily emerges, he was fully aware of his success in doing so.

Report of June 29, 1917, to the Bureau of Investigation, US Department of Justice, *in re* Max Gerlach, German Activities

Gerlach's escape from Berlin in the uncertain early days of World War I was a story of which he could be proud—and apparently also talk about after his return to America.[21] But by the middle of 1917 the situation had changed drastically for German-Americans in the United States. The invasion of Belgium and the alleged German atrocities in 1914, the sinking of the *Lusitania* on May 7, 1915, the resumption of unrestricted submarine warfare by the Germans after February 1, 1917, and other alarming events had combined to bring about widespread and strident anti-German hysteria. One aspect of this *Furor Americanus,* as it has been called (Wittke 163), was the formation of the American Protective League, a large group of volunteers organized to assist the Justice Department in collecting information about German-Americans suspected of spying and sabotage or of simply engaging in "German activities" and showing evidence of disloyalty. Like countless other German immigrants and German-Americans, Gerlach did not escape their notice. While there was no question in 1914 that his act of securing an American passport had betokened allegiance to the United States, his German background was beginning to count against him now that, as of April 6, 1917, the two nations actually were at war. According to a report prepared on June 29, 1917, by H. W. Grunewald, Gerlach was alleged "to have made some pro-German remarks" and to have "boasted that he was a personal friend of Major Ryan who was with Ambassador Gerard in Berlin in 1914": "Gerlach is supposed to have said that he had gotten Major Ryan drunk and thereby secured a passport." For good measure, a piece of information was appended that was beginning to take on a truly sinister aspect: "The informant also stated that Gerlach's father was a lieutenant in the German Army."

Again circumstances forced Gerlach to restyle his past, and again he was successful in doing so. Caught in the apparent dilemma between loyalty to his German background and ancestry on the one hand and commitment to what seems to be an ambitious and enterprising life in his adopted country

REPORT MADE BY:	PLACE WHERE MADE	DATE WHEN MADE	PERIOD FOR WHICH MADE
H. W. Grunewald	New York City	June 29-17	June 28
TITLE OF CASE AND OFFENSE CHARGED OR NATURE OF MATTER UNDER INVESTIGATION			
IN RE MAX GERLACH			
German Activities.			

RECEIVED
JUL 3 '917
Bureau of Investigation
DEPARTMENT OF JUSTICE

STATEMENT OF OPERATIONS, EVIDENCE COLLECTED, NAMES AND ADDRESSES OF PERSONS INTERVIEWED, PLACES VISITED, ETC.

This A.M. I proceeded to 700 Broadway to locate one Max Gerlach who was alleged to have made some pro-German remarks and who boasted that he was a personal friend of Major Ryan who was with Ambassador Gerard in Berlin in 1914. Gerlach is supposed to have said that he had gotten Major Ryan drunk and thereby secured a passport. The informant also states that Gerlach's father was a lieutenant in the German Army.

Gerlach could not be located at 700 Broadway. I then learned that Gerlach could be found at 141 W. 58th St. Gerlach stated that he was born October 12, 1885 in Yonkers, N.Y.; father and mother born in Germany. His father was a Lieutenant in the German Army but died about 27 years ago, and his mother married one Thomas Rile Gerlach was in Berlin in 1913 and left Berlin, Germany on a passport issued by Ambassador Gerard, August 14, 1914, then proceeded to London, England and here stayed about three weeks, then left for Boston, Mass. Gerlach showed me the German passport and also a personal card of Major Ryan who was staying at the "Kaiserhof" in Berlin, Germany. Major Ryan wrote on the face of it: "This will introduce Max Gerlach. He is O.K. Major Ryan." Gerlach also stated that he is a personal friend of one Captain Rice in the U. S. Army. Gerlach states that his cousin is in the 71st Regiment and that he himself is ready to do his bit. Nothing could be learned that would show that Major Ryan issued the passport or that he had fraudulently obtained the German passport, or that had any German connection in this country. Nothing could be learned that would show that Gerlach was pro-German, although it is advisable not to issue any passport for Gerlach should he ever request one owing to most of his relativ

COPY OF THIS REPORT FURNISHED TO:

-2-

OL 33016

8. 1917 Bureau of Investigation report *in re* Max Gerlach. National Archives and Records Administration. Footnote.com image.

on the other, Gerlach now chose his very own way of demonstrating unconditional allegiance to the United States: He responded to the challenge by deciding to style himself an American by birth and flatly stated that he "was born October 12, 1885 in Yonkers, N.Y.; father and mother born in Germany." He readily admitted that "his father was a Lieutenant in the German Army," but emphasized that he "died about 27 years ago," a date not quite accurate, as has been shown.

Gerlach was equally successful in dispelling the charge of having fraudulently obtained his passport, although there is sufficient evidence in the very application to point to a number of irregularities. For one thing, there is a reference to "the accompanying Certificate of Naturalization" of his mother, which he had obviously not been able to produce. In fact, its very absence is the reason for his giving the wrong dates of their immigration. Similarly, the vital passage certifying Gerlach's identity with the person referred to in said Certificate of Naturalization is left blank. Moreover, Gerlach freely admits to having fraternized with Major Ryan, probably in the classy Hotel Kaiserhof where the latter was staying, showing Ryan's card with the following inscription: "This will introduce Max Gerlach. He is O.K. Major Ryan." Further, the application was completed on August 3, 1914, but was re-dated as August 4, 1914, when it was signed by Harvey, the second secretary. And in addition to the incorrect year of birth, there were two inadvertent inconsistencies concerning the date of Gerlach's travel. However, some of these irregularities may well be due to the confusion vividly described by Ambassador Gerard as having prevailed in the embassy in the early weeks of the war and the embassy's extraordinary endeavor to assist the large number of those asking for help (see Gerard, *My Four Years in Germany*, chapter 10, "The Americans at the Outbreak of Hostilities").

Another feature in Gerlach's effort to confirm his loyalty as an American citizen and to deny German contacts in the United States is his strategy of bringing into play his connections with people of prominent social status. In addition to presenting Major Ryan's card and showing his passport as "issued by Ambassador Gerard," thus producing the name of a person much talked about in the months prior to America's entry into the war, Gerlach informed Grunewald, the investigator, "that he is a personal friend of one Captain Rice in the US Army." This was a name familiar at the time as that of an adventurer-soldier whose exploits go back to his having served as an officer in the Spanish-American and Philippine wars, and a name, moreover, that will reappear in Gerlach's biography. To dispel further the allegations raised against him, Gerlach "states that his cousin is in the 71st Regiment" and adds that he himself "is ready to do his bit."

Gerlach's Application of August 1918 for Service in the Ordnance Department, US Army

Gerlach's readiness "to do his bit" as well as his unequivocal commitment to the cause of the United States is clearly evident in his application for service in the US Army. Gerlach applied for a captain's commission in the Ordnance Department. His previous employment and activities would seem to constitute an excellent recommendation, quite unlike his ethnic background, however. While being a German by birth would not necessarily have precluded his entry into US military service, it would probably have impaired the chances of his application for an officer's commission. As he had begun to do in his response to the allegations of pro-German remarks, therefore, he again stated that he was born in Yonkers rather than in Germany. In addition to providing a survey of his education and a list of previous employers and occupations, which is incomplete for lack of space, Gerlach once more decided to offer the names of prominent people as references. First on the list is Major Cushman A. Rice, followed by the Honorable Aaron J. Levy, a judge, and George Young Bauchle, a lawyer, all of New York City. The strategy failed in the case of Levy, who informed Joseph Brennan of the American Protective League, the person assigned to investigate Gerlach's case, that he "does not know the subject [. . .]. Does not recall ever having heard the name mentioned" (1). While Cushman Rice was already serving in the US Army and could not be consulted, Mr. Bauchle gave Gerlach the highest commendation. As Brennan noted in his report of October 1, 1918: "According to Mr. Bauchle, subject suggests being an excellent mechanic, with thorough knowledge of automobiles and their mechanism. In the opinion of Mr. Bauchle, the subject's brain is so filled with mechanics that he is incapable of giving subtle thought to underhand work of any kind" (3). This did not satisfy Brennan, however, who had also learned from Bauchle that Gerlach had shown "casually, a personally autographed photo with writing on it in German characters, which had been presented to his father or grand-

9. Max Stork Gerlach, 1918 application for service, US Army, Ordnance Department. National Archives and Records Administration II, College Park, Maryland.

father, by Richard Wagner, the composer" (2). In his patriotic ardor, which mildly hints at the excesses that anti-German sentiments had reached by the end of 1918, the investigator concluded that he had "been unable to establish anything that would benefit the subject" (4) and that the "list of references appears camouflage. [. . .] There should rest grave suspicion on entire bona fides of Applicant" (5). While the report did not actually harm Gerlach, who had been appointed First Lieutenant on August 15, 1918, and sworn his oath of allegiance on October 1, 1918 (Index Card for Max Gerlach), it demonstrates the need for him, in his false claim to being an American citizen by birth, to continue to be cautious in performing the role he had chosen.

Gerlach's November 15, 1919, Application for a US Passport

After successful completion of his service in the Ordnance Department and his honorable discharge on October 31, 1919, Gerlach immediately applied for a US passport to travel to Havana, Cuba, for a two-month vacation.[23] The application is on a Form for Native Citizens, and Max S. Gerlach did not hesitate to "solemnly swear" that he was "born in Yonkers in the State of New York" on "the 12th day of October 1885." The questions that followed this incorrect answer required additional adjustments and manipulation of facts. Disregarding, here as elsewhere (except in his current middle name), the fact that it was in the company of his stepfather, Andrew Stork, that he had entered the United States, Gerlach proceeded to assert that it was his actual father, Ferdinand Gerlach, who had immigrated by way of the port of Glasgow, Scotland, and that this had happened around February 1884. Moving the date of immigration from 1894 to 1884 was necessary for Gerlach's birth to appear to have occurred in America. Gerlach further stated that Ferdinand Gerlach "resided about 3 years, uninterruptedly, in the United States, from 1884 to 1887, in New York," and that he had "died about 1887," which is in fact the probable date of his death, albeit in Germany, which he had never left.

Further manipulations were needed to conceal his extended visit to Germany in 1914, along with his hasty departure. Both were details that Gerlach may have considered detrimental to his plans at a time when the bitter war between the two nations had just ended. Answering the question about residencies outside the United States, he stated that he had stayed in France and England from 1912 to 1913, omitting Germany altogether. And the answer to the final question about where his last passport was obtained and how it was disposed of, is written in a different hand, helping Gerlach to tell another white lie: "never except Embassy passport issued 1913 now lost." In the same handwriting, apparently to authenticate the full range of statements made by Gerlach, there is a notice written across the face of the

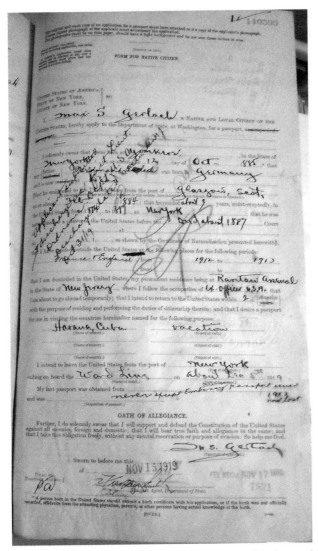

10a. Max S. Gerlach, front of 1919 application for US passport. National Archives and Records Administration II, College Park, Maryland.

page that would seem to have helped resolve all his loyalty difficulties, present and future: "Applicant submitted discharge First Lieut. Ordnance Dept. USA. Discharge dated Metuchen, N.J. Oct. 31 / 19."

For the "Affidavit of Identifying Witness" on the reverse side of the application, Gerlach called on none other than Major Rice, whose name had served twice earlier to authenticate and promote his interests. In view of the role

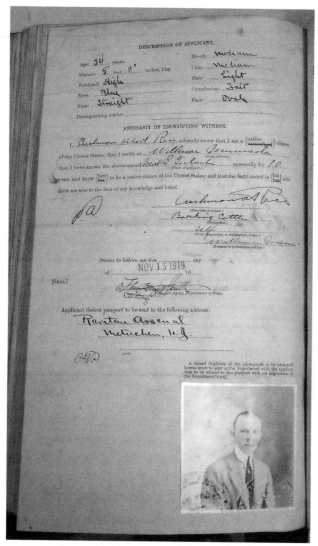

10b. Max S. Gerlach, back of 1919 application for US Passport. National Archives and Records Administration II, College Park, Maryland.

that Rice played in Gerlach's biography, the affidavit, written in Rice's hand, deserves to be quoted *in toto*: "I, Cushman Albert Rice, solemnly swear that I am a native citizen of the United States; that I reside at Wilmar, Minnesota; that I have known the above-named Max S. Gerlach personally for ten years and know him to be a native citizen of the United States; and that the facts stated in his affidavit are true to the best of my knowledge and belief.

(signed) Cushman A. Rice / (Occupation:) Banking Cattle / (Firm:) self / (Address:) Wilmar, Minn."

The 1919 passport application is the final document in a series that testifies to Gerlach's continued endeavor to present versions of his life that appeared amenable to the authorities involved and illustrate his constant need to negotiate the claims of the two cultures that had determined his biography. In this latter respect his experience exemplifies that of any immigrant, caught as he tends to be in the dilemma of divided loyalties, whether actual or imagined. For Gerlach, however, the case was manifestly exacerbated by an outright war between the two nations involved, as well as the pressure and hostilities resulting from agitation directed against people with a German background as well as against German institutions and German traditions in the United States. In a war that was waged against the German Kaiser and his Army, a man whose father was known to have held a position under that Kaiser's father or grandfather and to have served as a lieutenant in that army must have felt under particular duress to resolve the conflict. It is this aspect that makes Gerlach's biography interesting, beyond being simply an immigrant's case history of Americanization. Whatever additional obstacles and personal objectives may have been involved, however, by the time of his honorable discharge from the US Army Gerlach had managed to resolve all such conflicts successfully.

A passport photo attached to Gerlach's 1919 application is of altogether emblematic quality. It shows an almost ideal version of the Arrow Collar Man: a well-groomed Max Gerlach with a handkerchief in the pocket of his perfectly fitting jacket, wearing a shirt with a modish rounded collar and a dark tie with, in prominent display, a stick pin proclaiming his membership in the newly founded American Legion.[24] The German immigrant, thus, had become the American ex-officer and war veteran. More than that, he had passed through the war and military service as a sort of "purification rite" and in the process reinvented himself as an American, as a citizen not by immigration and naturalization but by actual birth. He had, in fact, ceased to be a hyphenated American. Having received his honorable discharge, he was now all but ready to face the world of the twenties: 34 years old, 5 foot 11 inches tall, of high forehead, blue eyes, straight nose, light hair, and fair complexion, to quote salient points from the Description of the Applicant. However, there is no mention as yet of Max Gerlach as Max *von* Gerlach, no hint

11. Max S. Gerlach, 1919 passport photo. National Archives and Records Administration II, College Park, Maryland.

of the German nobility predicate that was part of his name when the Fitzgeralds met him (according to Zelda's memory of Gerlach in 1947) as "a neighbor named von Guerlach or something who was said to be General Pershing's nephew and was in trouble over bootlegging," in Henry Dan Piper's wording.

Further Self-Stylizations of Max Gerlach

In terms of Gerlach's self-stylization, shedding the liability of a foreign birth and emerging as an American ex-officer and a war veteran appears to have been the ultimate achievement in his Americanization. It comes as a surprise, therefore, that after the end of the war, when the *Furor Americanus* was subsiding, he began to claim and to use the German nobility predicate "von," not only a marker of social distinction but also an unambiguous marker of his ethnic origin. The Fitzgeralds apparently knew him solely as Max von Gerlach; one of the two charges of possessing and selling liquor brought forward against him in 1927 is against "Max V. Gerlach"; the 1939 newspaper reports of his suicide attempt refer to him as Max von Gerlach, as does a passenger list documenting his arrival at Idlewild on March 26, 1950. A 1951 letter to Mizener also is from Max von Gerlach, and when in 1954 Belle Trenholm wrote to Mizener, she did so again on behalf of Max von Gerlach, her letter including his calling card with that name printed on it. In all New York City telephone directories during the 1950s, he had himself listed as Max von Gerlach. Although on some official documents, as well as on his tombstone, his name continued to be given as Max Stork Gerlach, he had actually begun

12. Max von Gerlach, calling card. Princeton University Library.

to cultivate an existence as the son of a German baron,[25] educated at some English university, and speaking with an Oxford accent—a person, moreover, who had served as a major rather than as a first lieutenant.[26] It is not at all impossible that, in an odd reversal of his impact on *The Great Gatsby*, it was his familiarity with the novel and knowledge of the part he had played in its composition that were responsible for certain aspects of the role he finally chose for himself, or that helped him to develop such aspects from whatever peculiarities of personality and bearing had fallen to his lot as a Teutonic-featured man of German descent. While he continued to cling to the nobility predicate with its implicit affirmation of his ethnicity, the liability of an association with Germany seems to have irked him once again after World War II. The official papers prepared by Frank E. Campbell, Inc., the funeral parlor in charge of his burial, indicate that Gerlach had begun to suggest Austria as the country of his origin (Gerlach Burial Records 1). This was a ploy frequently used at the time to explain a German family name and accent in order to escape the kind of censure that had been Gerlach's lot to suffer at the outset of the earlier war. In a way, then, the burden or the markers of his German ethnicity affected him to his very last years, oddly calling into question the initial success of his Americanization.

One purpose of the reconstruction of Gerlach's family history has been to assess his possible entitlement to the nobility predicate, with the result that the claim is plainly fraudulent. However, instances of this kind of ennoblement were by no means infrequent in the twenties. The glamor and notoriety surrounding people such as Paul von Hindenburg (Field Marshal during the war), Erich von Stroheim (the movie actor and director, himself a Viennese immigrant of middle-class origin), and the notorious Monsignore Rudolf von Gerlach (a Bavarian, of doubtful nobility himself, who at the beginning of the war enjoyed the protection of the Vatican to promote the interests of the Central Powers), for instance, could have served as an example and become an outright temptation for Max Gerlach to turn himself into a more glamorous Max von Gerlach. Moreover, there were prominent von Gerlachs in German and international politics as well as in the officers' corps of the German Army, whom he would have known of and who would have lent credibility to the combination of his name with the nobility predicate. At the same time, files in the National Archives and Records Administration show many people fraudulently styling themselves as members of the nobility, generally for criminal purposes. Allegations and charges were never for actually claiming the nobility-related predicate, however, which seems to have been a simple matter, but rather for criminal offenses committed while using it. And frequently it was the conflict of loyalty between the two nations that was the source of such offenses, at least in those cases where the Federal Bureau of Investigation saw a reason to become involved (see Card Index to Names of Persons in General Departmental Files, 1917–1930; and Box 151, PI-194 E-101 HM 1993, RG 60, General Records of the Department of Justice, the latter containing information on about 25 cases).

While it is futile to speculate about Max Gerlach's motivations for beginning to style himself as Max von Gerlach, there is no doubt that it helped give him social standing, in personal as well as business dealings, suggesting as it did the kind of affluence that Gerlach has been so readily credited with in scholarly and popular lore. Using the nobility predicate would have been especially helpful, for instance, if he should have continued to operate as an automobile broker selling to wealthy clients the more expensive types of cars with which he had been associated. While the long list of his occupations and positions in connection with automobiles had been an excellent recommendation for an officer's position in the Ordnance Department, his combined professional experience and patriotic service certainly gave him an impressive standing as a businessman at the outset of the prosperous twenties. Ennobling himself, additionally, constituted a supreme act of self-aggrandizement, an extension almost of the feat he had carried off by brashly proclaiming himself an American by birth. But in the final analysis Gerlach's self-ennoblement involved no less an act than the outright denial of his parents. Gerlach himself may have seen this—certainly his mother and family did—and so would such a discerning author as Fitzgerald if he was in a position to weigh all the facts as he was pondering the suitability of the Gerlach matter for the great American novel he was in the process of planning. And there is reason to believe that Fitzgerald did see this, for Jay Gatsby, his protagonist, too, will plainly disavow his ancestors: "he didn't believe that he was the son of his parents at all," as the author puts it in the manuscript version of his book (*MS* 216, see *RRG* 161).

F. Scott Fitzgerald and Max von Gerlach

Max von Gerlach's immigrant biography as a whole, along with a large number of its details and incidents, points to *The Great Gatsby* and suggests more clearly than ever the impact of Gerlach on the conception and writing of the novel. But where and how did Gerlach and the Fitzgeralds meet? And how did Fitzgerald learn about Gerlach's story? In answering these questions, great care is needed in order not to replace the untenable myth of Gerlach, the Long Island neighbor and wealthy gentleman bootlegger, with similarly unjustified constructions. None of the subsequent attempts to provide an answer can claim to be positive truth, therefore; they are simply attempts to fill in gaps in Gerlach's and Fitzgerald's biographies. These reasonable inferences proceed from the relatively few known facts that allow for different explanations of what is a certainty, however: Zelda's assertion that Gatsby was based on Gerlach.

Even if one no longer believes Gerlach to be the wealthy Long Island gentleman bootlegger that he has been supposed to be and does not actually identify him as a neighbor of the Fitzgeralds while they were living in Great Neck, one still has to account for three pieces of information about him that Zelda Fitzgerald presented as fact: his having been a "neighbor" after all, his having been "in trouble over bootlegging," and his having been "said to be General Pershing's nephew." The last rumor called for extended research, since it promised to provide reliable biographical information about Gerlach. In the end the search failed to establish the slightest hint of any link between the Gerlach and Pershing families. But it still turned up a number of details of particular relevance to Gerlach, Fitzgerald, and Jay Gatsby in relation to their interaction and interdependence. To begin with, there is the curious fact that on his 1942 World War II Draft Registration Card Max Gerlach gave as a "person who will always know your address," not the name of a member of his Gerlach or Stork families, but that of James F. Pershing of 17 East 55th Street, New York City (1). James Fletcher Pershing Jr., the son of General John J. Pershing's younger brother, was born in Chicago in 1891, served as infantry officer in the American Expeditionary Force in France, moved to New York City to become a member of a stock brokerage firm in the early 1920s, became known as a man "of character and ability" ("Blames Public . . ."), served as Assistant Prohibition Director for six months in 1922 before giving up the position as "distasteful" ("Pershing Quits Job . . ."), and was working for the Chelsea Management Corporation when Gerlach gave his name as reference. Pershing, through family connections and social standing, represents the kind of person with whom Gerlach, in his social aspirations, would have been eager to associate. But the actual reason for the trust that Gerlach put in Pershing emerges from information provided by an earlier document, the latter's World War I Draft Registration Card of June 5, 1917. It shows Pershing still residing in Chicago and working as "Automobile Parts Salesman" with the Fulton Sales Company at 910 South Michigan Avenue (1). It would appear that Gerlach and Pershing met while they were both living in Chicago and engaged in work connected with automobiles. So once again here is evidence that the story of Max Gerlach, in its relevance as inspiration for the protagonist of *The Great Gatsby,* touches on Gerlach's connection with automobiles and that it was Gerlach's personal and commercial interest in cars, in their maintenance and distribution, that determined his social contacts and circle of friends and acquaintances as it was to develop in the 1920s.

The seemingly accidental circumstance of the Gerlach-Pershing link also affects our assessment of the link between Gerlach and the Fitzgeralds, and finally that between Gerlach, the Fitzgeralds, and Jay Gatsby. Regardless of whether Zelda had either misunderstood or misrepresented the case of the supposed Gerlach-Pershing family relationship, or whether her account of it was perhaps misrepresented by Henry Dan Piper, to the Fitzgeralds Max Gerlach was certainly much more than a casual acquaintance. They learned enough about him to know about his association with James Fletcher Pershing Jr., the actual nephew of General John J. Pershing, which fact in turn gave rise to the rumor of Gerlach himself as the General's nephew. And it stands to reason that this particular rumor—one of the few things the Fitzgeralds are known to have known about Gerlach—should be reflected in *The Great Gatsby,* in the protagonist's being said to be "a nephew or a cousin of Kaiser Wilhelm's" (28) or "a nephew to von Hindenburg" (49), with either one of these uncles, ironically, representing the very enemy that Pershing had been fighting against in the Great War.

Zelda's statement that Gerlach was "in trouble over bootlegging" does not actually suggest major legal difficulties for him. Rather, it would seem to point to the kind of trouble he found himself in in 1927 when he pleaded guilty to charges of possessing and selling liquor (in relatively small quantities) as well as owning equipment for bottling alcohol.[27] The offense "hardly seems grand enough for the man who inspired the characterization of Jay Gatsby," as Bruccoli put it in connection with another violator by the name of Gerlach who was arrested in 1926 for possession of beer ("'How Are You and the Family Old Sport'—Gerlach and Gatsby" 35). That Zelda should mention this trouble at all can be for only two reasons: one, that it points to Jay Gatsby and his big-time bootleg activities as described in the novel; the other more likely reason is that it actually was in his capacity as a small-time bootlegger that she and her husband had known Gerlach. This latter possibility is supported by the fact that there were altogether three raids in succession at Gerlach's address, indicating that as a minor dealer he did not enjoy the protection of organized crime, which usually prevented such a procedure (see Pietrusza 207). And if his bootleg activities were hardly grand enough to have inspired the character of Jay Gatsby, it must have been something else about Gerlach that fascinated and influenced Fitzgerald, leaving the small-time bootleg activity to do no more than suggest a big-time bootlegging background to be borrowed (as it appears to have been) from Fleischmann and other Long Island people. Despite all of Gerlach's professional experience and know-how and their relevance to large-scale alcohol smuggling during the Prohibition years from 1920 to 1933—and allowing for involvement in other large-scale criminal activity and culminating in his being referred to as a "wealthy yachtsman" in the 1930 newspaper photo caption ("yachtsman" sometimes "a euphemism for rum-runner," as Bruccoli observed)—there is reason to believe, now that one must question Gerlach's status as a wealthy gentleman bootlegger, that this yachtsman's activity of his was simply that of an actual yachtsman.[28] As such it takes us back to the very beginnings of Gerlach's professional career as a marine gas engineer and at the same time points to his technical and commercial interest in automobile technology as his abiding preoccupation, in the twenties as much as earlier and afterward.

There are not a few people in Gerlach's life—such as Major Cushman A. Rice, the Honorable Aaron J. Levy, and George Young Bauchle, the three prominent references given in his officer's application, as well as other notables with whom he had rubbed shoulders—whose acquaintance suggests that he could have been tempted to seek shortcuts to success and wealth. But the most likely career path that Gerlach followed in the twenties seems to have involved automobiles. Major Rice, whom Gerlach had met in Cuba as early as 1909, pursued banking and cattle farming, but it was probably through his interest in the expensive automobiles that he owned in Cuba as well as in New York City[29] and Gerlach's interest in promoting auto racing in Cuba (see Ordnance Department Personalia Sheet) that they first met and continued to be in contact, before, during, and after the war. Judge Levy went on to become justice of the New York Supreme Court and majority leader of the New York State Assembly. He is known to have protected Manhattan gambling clubs and been involved "in 'producing' raid-free property" (Katcher 253; see also Pietrusza 207), but this occurred long after Gerlach named him as a reference and expected him to testify to his technical qualifications for service in the Ordnance Department. As it turned out, Levy did not remember Gerlach, probably because the latter had merely sold him an automobile. Bauchle, who gave Gerlach the most positive recommendation, went on to acquire notoriety and disgrace as a gambler, wastrel, and cohort of the infamous Arnold Rothstein, the model for Fitzgerald's Meyer Wolfsheim.[30] Despite what the criminal background of *The Great Gatsby* seems to suggest, however, Gerlach does not appear to have been implicated in any of these activities. In fact, as the history of composition of Fitzgerald's novel tells us, the author evidently borrowed from other sources to fill in this aspect of Gatsby and only did so long after he had first set up his protagonist. Gerlach, then, in keeping with the rationale that led him to choose the other two references, picked Bauchle because of the interest they shared in automobiles. And it is noteworthy that when Bauchle died in 1939, it was his role as an automobilist, rather than his conspicuous criminal career, that the obituary in the *New York Times* saw fit to emphasize: "At the time of the war and for a few years thereafter he was well known as a first-nighter, automobilist and patron of various sports" ("George Y. Bauchle").

There is good reason, therefore, to believe that it was automobiles and small-time bootlegging that brought Gerlach and the Fitzgeralds together in the early twenties. Either of these fields could easily have produced such a disagreement between them as Gerlach hints at in his correspondence with Mizener. Allowing for the possibility that Gerlach did get involved in illegal and even criminal operations by permitting his various contacts to draw him into deals of their own scheming, his returning to the field of automobiles and the wide scope of commercial activities it involved promised a bright future for him as the twenties were getting under way. Fitzgerald, as the decade's exemplary spokesman, was also an exemplary consumer and potential customer. It was a mere month after he and Zelda were married on April 3, 1920, and when they had moved from the Biltmore to the Commodore in Manhattan, that Scott bought his first car, a fashionable secondhand Marmon. It was this car that took them to Westport, Connecticut, in May 1920, where they rented the Wakeman House on Compo Road until the fall of that year. His *Ledger* for the same month records "Car broken," and in June he again notes, "Car troubles" (174). On July 15 the Fitzgeralds motored to Montgomery, Alabama, with much difficulty, and then sold what had proved to be an unreliable vehicle, returning to Westport by train in August. A somewhat fictionalized account of the journey, "The Cruise of the Rolling Junk," was published in three installments in *Motor* magazine in the spring of 1924. The article was illustrated with a series of staged photos of Scott and Zelda, a new car having taken the couple back to familiar sights in Westport as well as other locations in 1923. In a biographical sketch of the same year, the author is quoted as entertaining what appear to be two thoroughly characteristic wishes: "I would like to have an awful lot of money with which to buy all the books I want and a Rolls-Royce car" (B. F. Wilson 420). He did, in fact, get to own the Rolls-Royce, even though the premium car he owned turned out once again to be a secondhand model.

Gerlach worked for various automobile dealers and also sold vehicles as a broker, apparently providing cars for discriminating customers (such as Rice, Levy, and Bauchle) and finding customers for the more exclusive makes of cars that he was promoting. Having returned from Cuba on March 9, 1920, he could well have served the Fitzgeralds when early in May, while in the company of Leon Ruth, a friend from their Montgomery days, the couple went shopping for their first vehicle. As Ruth recalls: "Neither of them could drive much. Scott used to borrow my car in Montgomery when he was courting Zelda, so I knew fairly well the limits of his ability. As I remember it we went down to the Battery, and it was a choice between a new sedan and a secondhand Marmon sports coupe. Of course, they couldn't resist the Marmon. Well, we bought it and I drove them up to 125th Street. I showed Scott how to shift on the way and both of them knew something about steering. Then they put me out and struck off" (qtd. in Lewis 1). The "car troubles" were probably largely due to Scott's and Zelda's negligence about driving as well as in taking care of the Marmon, particularly Zelda's "completely de-intestining it" when she "drove it over a fire-plug" (Lewis 1) in Westport. But Zelda, in retrospect, put the blame on "a man [who] sold us a broken Marmon" (*My Lost City* 304), and Scott, of course, had dubbed the car a "rolling junk." The various troubles must have necessitated contact with the person who had actually sold them what had at first appeared to be a classy coupe. This is how Gerlach could have become their "neighbor," soon proving a convenient source to fill their liquor needs as well, and a supplier, perhaps, of the automobile that was needed for the 1923 photo shoot, apparently a Nash touring car (Bruccoli, "Introduction," *The Cruise of the Rolling Junk* n5).

Having their acquaintance begin at such an early point on the road to *The Great Gatsby* could explain a number of the correlations to be noted between the novel and incidents in Gerlach's life following his return to civilian life after the war. By the time of the writing of *The Great Gatsby,* thus, the Gerlach-

Fitzgerald acquaintance would have lasted long enough to allow for the familiar "old sport" salutation of the summer of 1923 (to be used by Gerlach as a correspondent who had since ceased to be a "neighbor") as well as, more importantly, to provide occasions for Gerlach to share versions of his somewhat uncommon biography with Fitzgerald. In fact, Barbara Probst Solomon's much-acclaimed 1996 essay "Westport Wildlife" and a few other contributions from local historians have argued that *The Great Gatsby* owes more to Westport than it does to Great Neck. While bootleg alcohol is known to have played a major role in the social life of Westport in the early twenties, and certainly in that of the Fitzgeralds as well, the actual name of Gerlach, however, had not surfaced as yet.[31] But there is another likely occasion for contact between Gerlach and the Fitzgeralds, when in mid-October 1922, after an extended absence from the East, the couple took up residence at 6 Gateway Drive in Great Neck on Long Island and Scott went ahead and bought his secondhand Rolls-Royce, "the most autonomous automobile on Long Island," as novelist and critic Ernest Boyd remarked (qtd. in Mizener, *The Far Side of Paradise* 151). Again, this was the kind of car that Gerlach would have been associated with, and again this (as much as the Compo Road address in Westport had been) was a location where the Fitzgeralds were much in need of an efficient supplier of bootleg alcohol[33]—a person to stay anonymous and never show up as a guest at the countless functions his services helped to enhance, a person not ever to be found in the photos that have survived of such occasions.

These speculations about the possible circumstances of the Fitzgerald-Gerlach link, while they proceed from actual facts in the biographies of the people concerned and from Zelda's memory of Gerlach and his role in the composition of *The Great Gatsby,* as well as from the reflection of such facts in the novel itself, nonetheless would seem to find only vague additional substantiation, to begin with, in references in Fitzgerald's writings of the period. His novel *The Beautiful and Damned,* which was in great part written during the couple's Westport residence and draws heavily on their experiences there, dramatizes events that involve their Marmon and other automobiles as well as their alcoholic indulgences and excesses. But there are no specifics that clearly point to Gerlach. Speculations about Tana, their Japanese houseboy, as "a German agent kept in this country to disseminate Teutonic propaganda through Westchester County" (199) could reflect the suspicions regarding Gerlach's being involved in pro-German activities. But they are, in fact, traceable to a hoax concocted by George Jean Nathan, editor of *The Smart Set* and, along with Edmund Wilson, one of the group of friends who attended their Westport revels in the summer of 1920. Fitzgerald's play, *The Vegetable,* a "caricature of the American dream and its political system" (Scribner 20), set and written in 1922, has in it a bootlegger named Snooks who personally delivers contraband alcohol to his customers and takes telephone orders as Gerlach may have done. But as a character he is totally unlike Gerlach. Zelda's 1932 novel *Save Me the Waltz* in part covers the same period and mentions drunken automobile rides along the Boston Post Road, speakeasies, New York City bars, and also the secondhand Marmon. But characters in it who seem to be in any way close to Gerlach appear to have other real-life models. The *Gatsby* cluster stories of 1922 and 1923 in their established relatedness to the novel similarly contain references to automobiles and bootleggers. But none of them point to Gerlach as their exclusive source. In fact, while Gerlach himself must have been around in the lives of the Fitzgeralds, it was not until the writing of the story "Absolution," in the summer of 1923, that his influence became apparent. "Absolution," as Fitzgerald explained, was evolved from material of an abandoned early draft of *The Great Gatsby.* And so it is safe to conclude that Fitzgerald actually came to perceive the potential of the Gerlach matter at the very moment when his initial idea in 1922 for a novel set in "the middle west and New York of 1885," "centered on a smaller period of time," and having "a catholic element" (*Life in Letters* 60) was given up and the author began to approach his material from "a new angle," as he informed Maxwell Perkins, his editor at Scribner's, in April 1924 (*Letters* 162). "Absolution," according to Fitzgerald, was to have functioned as a kind of prologue to *The Great Gatsby.* But when the author decided to preserve the sense of mystery surrounding the protagonist, the matter became dispensable. As an independent story published in *The American Mercury,* it is a substantial contribution to the author's oeuvre and anticipates central aspects of the novel, such as the German immigrant background of the protagonist, the drab circumstances of his Midwestern childhood, his dreams about a more glorious future, and his name change to signal rejection of the past, as well as such physical aspects as the brilliance of his blue eyes. All of these traits in their interrelatedness, while owing much to literary models such as James Joyce's *Dubliners,* are closely related to Max Gerlach's story. Gerlach, then, as the evidence would seem to indicate, was the "one man I knew," as Fitzgerald put it, to start off the protagonist of *The Great Gatsby,* before he later changed into Fitzgerald himself (*Letters* 358).

Gerlach and/in *The Great Gatsby*

As a writer well known to complain about his lack of suitable material for a novel[34] and as someone who felt that he had completely exhausted the material of his own life in his earlier novels, Fitzgerald must have been an attentive listener to Gerlach's story and also have come to recognize the suitability and the value of Gerlach's immigrant experience as subject matter for the impressive and ambitious contribution to American literature that he wanted his next novel to be. This occurred at a time when Theodore Dreiser and other literary models were helping Fitzgerald to shape his idea of such a work, and when, in the interview cited in connection with his desire to own a Rolls-Royce car, he emphatically stated, "I consider H. L. Mencken and Theodore Dreiser the greatest men living in the country today" (B. F. Wilson 420). This assertion echoes lines in a June 3, 1920, letter to President John Grier Hibben of Princeton University: "My view of life, President Hibben, is the view of Theodore Driesers and Joseph Conrads—that life is too strong and remorseless for the sons of men" (*Life in Letters* 40). These words are borrowed from Hugh Walpole's evaluation of Conrad, as quoted in Mencken's essay on "Theodore Dreiser" in *A Book of Prefaces* (1916), and reflect the impact of Mencken's counsel.[35] Add to these heroes and models the German philosopher Friedrich Nietzsche and the German general and military strategist Erich Ludendorff (whose names appear in discussions of Fitzgerald's reading during the twenties [36]), as well as the German historian and philosopher Oswald Spengler (author of *The Decline of the West*), of whom Fitzgerald later somewhat inaccurately claimed, "I read him the same summer I was writing 'The Great Gatsby' and I don't think I ever quite recovered from him" (*Letters* 289–90),[37] and one can readily see why a man of Max von Gerlach's stature, with his German background and peculiar immigrant experience, should have been of interest to Fitzgerald: all of these writers, in an abstract fashion, were focusing on constituent elements of Gerlach as a type.

Dreiser in particular "was quite simply Fitzgerald's measuring stick of greatness," as Thomas P. Riggio has suggested (235). Following Maxwell Geismar's and Eric Solomon's earlier observations regarding Fitzgerald's possible indebtedness to a story by the older writer, the critic goes on to build a strong case for Dreiser's poignant account of Joseph G. Robin né Rabinovitch in "'Vanity, Vanity,' Saith the Preacher," the ninth item in his collection *Twelve Men* (1919), as an inspiration for *The Great Gatsby*. He also makes a convincing case for "W. L. S.," the final sketch in that volume, to have provided "cadences and images" for the ending of Fitzgerald's novel (240). There is a suggestion, in Riggio's reasoning, that Fitzgerald "may have felt anxious in part because he had [. . .] found in Dreiser sources for his writing" and that it was for that reason that he openly "told friends that Gatsby was based on a Long Island bootlegger whom he had met" (238). While this final point is no longer a persuasive argument, it is true that in view of his admiration for the older author Fitzgerald must have been pleased to find in Gerlach an authentic person with an authentic story as a model for telling his own variation of the kind of American tragedy that was Dreiser's literary domain, giving Fitzgerald an opportunity to work, as Dreiser had done in all twelve sketches in his collection, from unfortunate real-life prototypes.[38] Thus, Gerlach not merely helped Fitzgerald evade possible charges of being overly indebted to Dreiser, but also, and more importantly perhaps, appeared on the scene as member of an ethnic group whose merits and role in world history were matters of interest in then-current social philosophy and historiography, as well as in the author's own thinking along such lines. Mencken had helped Fitzgerald develop a pro-German attitude, which led him to read and appreciate Nietzsche and Ludendorff. The racial implications of their writings seemed to appeal to Fitzgerald, whose concern about his own ethnic heritage as a Celt was becoming a matter of record.[39] During his first visit to Europe in 1921, Fitzgerald went to Oxford and embraced the place in all its literary associations. Returning there after brief visits to France and Rome, he perceived on High Street the shadows of the Via Appia and famously mused,

"In how many years would our descendents approach this ruin with supercilious eyes to buy postcards from men of a short, inferior race—a race that once were Englishmen" ("Three Cities," *FSF in His Own Time* 126). This pondering anticipates the tenor of what was to fascinate Fitzgerald about Spengler's *The Decline of the West,* in the popular misunderstanding of its title (in early newspaper and magazine responses) as referring to an imminent doom rather than to the slow process of transformation that, in the view of Spengler, takes each indigenous culture through the stages of childhood, youth, manhood, and old age. Decline and dissipation such as Fitzgerald had perceived in the works of Dreiser as well as of Conrad, Hardy, Charles G. and Frank Norris, and other novelists whom he praised had been a thematic undercurrent in his own work as early as *The Beautiful and Damned.* The loss of belief in the power of political ideals to determine the fate of man and to curb his innate rapacity had informed *The Vegetable* as well as such cautionary tales as "May Day" and "The Diamond as Big as the Ritz." *The Great Gatsby* was to take the story to its bitter end, making the telling of it all the more poignant by invoking throughout—and famously in its ending—the American Dream in the infinite promises of its ideal. By having Gatsby represent the nation as a whole, the novel is, in fact, the correlative in literature of Spengler's narrative of Western culture being degraded in materialism. It compresses the extended process described by Spengler into the relatively short space of a man's life, from youthful dreams to their corruption and destruction. The cultural pessimism brought on by the experience of the Great War, first to be perceived when the initial fervent backing of its cause begins to die (as shown in "May Day"), induces the corruption of the American Dream in the materialism of the twenties: the ideal cannot survive the withdrawal of its unanimous and unrestrained support.

The important thing to note about Fitzgerald's use of Gerlach as a model for his protagonist is that unlike Dreiser's sketches and the various other literary sources that, consciously or unconsciously, Fitzgerald drew on in the writing of *The Great Gatsby*, the story of Max von Gerlach was not as readily available to him, either in its entirety or as a definitive record. Rather, it was a story that (apart from vague hearsay perhaps) Fitzgerald could only learn about, bit by bit, from none other than Gerlach himself, over a long period—a long enough period, in fact, to have Fitzgerald and Gerlach reach the degree of familiarity that would bring about the "old sport" salutation, however lightly spoken. Whatever the actual circumstances, the process would need to have begun with Gerlach as he first appeared to Fitzgerald—perhaps a person of "some undefined consequence" (a term used in an insert on galley 20 [*RRG* 51]), with the "von" acting as an ethnic as well as a social marker, an attribute attracting attention as well as curiosity—and it would have gone on to uncover such aspects of Gerlach's past as the latter chose to reveal. Given the conflicting versions of the spurious biographies previously devised by him, it would have either laid bare or at least hinted at certain contradictions, and of necessity the conflicting versions would have been resolved (if perhaps only in the author's imagination and in what he intuited about Gerlach) in the exonerating climax of a rhetorical question: "[. . .] what better right has an imaginative man got than to invent his own past"—the question mark missing, for possible emphasis. This conclusion, as it stands in the manuscript of the novel (*MS* 216), appeared important enough to the author to warrant revision and transcendence in the rewritten galleys: "[. . .] what better right does a man possess than to invent his own antecedents?" (*RRG* 161). At the same time, leaving the immediate confines of Gerlach's story but still building on it, the author has Gatsby arrive at the outright denial of his parents: "he didn't believe he was the son of his parents at all" (*MS* 216, see *RRG* 161). The sentence echoes Fitzgerald's early belief about himself, as much as it reflects the moving story of Joseph G. Rabinovitch as told by Dreiser, providing sufficient reason to pique Fitzgerald's interest in what was Gerlach's particular version of rewriting one's biography and in what were his motives in doing so. But it is the passage following the rhetorical question in its two variants that really matters and that alone (in slight modification) was to survive into the printed text: "Jay Gatsby of West Egg, Long Island sprang from his platonic conception of himself. From nothing else. He was a son of God—a phrase which, if it means anything at all, means just that. His family were less than nothing to him; he must be about his Father's business, which ^was the service of^ a vast, vulgar ^and metricious^ beauty ~~of America~~, and to ^that^ was faithful until the end" (*MS* 216, see *RRG* 161–62 and *GG* 77).

Central as it is to the novel, and coming as it does from an immigrant, the passage stands as the actual Max Gerlach's preeminent contribution to the

"No, I studied there — for six months. Perhaps you remember that a lot of American officers were given a chance to go there just after the war."

For some reason I wanted to slap him on the back but now suddenly he was telling me a lot of things. He had juxtaposed various events, he said, to make people wonder; his family were poor but he had inherited money, or almost inherited it and the reason he had invented a golden spoon for himself was because he didn't believe he was the son of his parents at all.

This sounds like a shoddy remark but it simply wasn't. I was absolutely sure what he meant — the fact that he was born in indisputable wedlock had never convinced his imagination and what better right has an imaginative man got than to invent his own past. Jay Gatsby of West Egg, Long Island sprang from his platonic conception of himself. From nothing else. He was a son of god — a phrase which, if it means anything at all, means just that. His family were less than nothing to him; he must be about his father's business, which a vast, vulgar, beauty of america, and to that was faithful until the end.

13. Detail from *The Great Gatsby,* manuscript chapter 7, p. 2. Reproduced from *"The Great Gatsby": A Facsimile of the Manuscript,* p. 216.

conception of *The Great Gatsby* and clearly takes the work beyond anything suggested by Dreiser's example. Max Gerlach—having lost his German father, a second lieutenant in the Prussian Army, at the age of two; arriving in the United States under a different name as an immigrant at the age of nine; following the career of a self-made man; reclaiming, in the course of his career, his original name; styling himself as an American by birth; entering the US Army to become an officer, then a veteran, and a member of the American Legion; and ennobling himself by affixing the German nobility predicate to his family name and thus rejecting his commoner's heritage—had invented aspects of his past and restyled aspects of his personality in quest of an ideal, which (in Fitzgerald's imaginative use of those biographical details in the characterization of his protagonist) ultimately emerged as nothing less than the American Dream. While Fitzgerald defines Gatsby's business as "the service of a vast, vulgar and meretricious beauty" to account for its cheapening in the twenties, he adds (and afterward deletes as redundant) the words "of America" in an attempt to underscore (as Dreiser was to do in *An American Tragedy*) the national aspect of the story that was of paramount interest to him in transforming Gerlach's immigrant case history into a narrative for which, as a consequence, he was to find the title "Under the Red, White, and Blue" actually to be more appropriate than that of *The Great Gatsby* (see Bruccoli, "Appendix 2: Note on the Title," *GG* 206–08).

As readily emerges, then, Gerlach's impact on the thematic concerns of *The Great Gatsby* was immense, easily absorbing all specific details that can be traced to him. At the same time, there is another aspect of the novel that equally demonstrates the importance of the encounter between Fitzgerald and Gerlach, for the course of composition as much as for the final shape of the work: that of narrative technique. I would argue that the process of learning ever more about Gerlach's life and personality turned out to provide the basic structural device of the novel, governing Fitzgerald's writing of the manuscript as well as, in the finished product, his narrator's growing perception of the protagonist, culminating in the latter's ultimate defense: "You're worth the whole damn bunch put together" (*GG* 120). In all probability, this process of getting to know Gerlach is reflected—and perhaps even deliberately or inadvertently hinted at—in the manuscript of *The Great Gatsby* in a brief passage on page 2 that was canceled immediately after it had been written: "Little by little, for ^he was not^ one of those men who make general confessions, I came to know more about Gatsby than anyone else ever knew. And in telling the story of that summer on Long Island I shall let him drift into it casually, *as he did in life*, without suspicion that he would come to dominate it—that he who walked so lightly ~~shout~~ would be the only one to leave footprints in that vacuum after all" (*MS* 3; emphasis added). His seeming presumptuousness of addressing Fitzgerald as "old sport" notwithstanding, Gerlach is reported to have been as reserved as Gatsby is shown to be in the early chapters of the novel. In the first newspaper account of his suicide at-

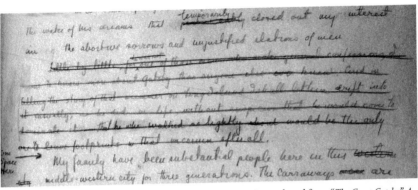

14. Detail from *The Great Gatsby*, manuscript chapter 1, p. 2. Reproduced from *"The Great Gatsby": A Facsimile of the Manuscript*, p. 3.

tempt in 1939, for instance, the police is quoted as saying "that Gerlach was not given to talking about his past, his relatives or his personal affairs and, aside from the report that he has a wife somewhere, they had no knowledge of whether he has relatives in this country or abroad" ("Car Dealer Dying" 2). Fitzgerald's deletion of the above passage is in accordance with his decision to present events dramatically, by "showing" rather than by "telling," and also serves "to preserve the sense of mystery," as he put it in a 1934 letter to John Jamieson (*Letters* 509).

Another stage in the process of getting acquainted with Gerlach and writing about him is similarly reflected at a point in the manuscript when Fitzgerald may have realized (as he later confessed) that as a person Gerlach did not meet his expectations as a protagonist and, therefore, had to be filled with Fitzgerald's own emotional life. As Nick Carraway explains, "I had talked with him perhaps half a dozen times in the past month and found, to my disappointment, that he had little to say" (*MS* 269 insert). Further bits of information continue to be given—some the result of later revisions suggested by Maxwell Perkins (*Life in Letters* 87)—and to help strike a balance between revealing and withholding facts about Gerlach and his biography. This balance prevails for much of the novel and not only helps the narrator "reserve all judgements" (*GG* 5) to the end, but also gives the story its basic suspense. As in the case of Gerlach's impact on the theme of the novel, where Fitzgerald's own planning found support in the example of Dreiser, so, too, was

Gerlach's influence on the development of Fitzgerald's narrative technique similarly supported by literary example, that of Joseph Conrad before all others. And Conrad's mentorship was fully acknowledged, too: "God! I've learned a lot from him," is what Fitzgerald told Mencken shortly after the publication of *The Great Gatsby* (*Letters* 482).

The above reassessment of the role of Gerlach in the conception of the theme of *The Great Gatsby,* as well as of its basic structure, finds its complement in the diminished importance of Gerlach's role as a bootlegger in the 1924 manuscript of the novel. References to bootlegging would now seem to appear in a different light: it was not Gatsby as a wealthy bootlegger that Fitzgerald was interested in, but Gatsby as a dreamer of the American Dream. Therefore, a certain vagueness as to Gatsby's activities seemed acceptable, even called for. So while bootlegging is hinted at as his source of income (his only source of income to begin with), he is a bootlegger chiefly because he is rumored to be one by his party guests or taken to be one by Jordan Baker and Tom Buchanan. Along with other details of Gatsby's life, references to actual bootleg activities are kept in the background, supporting, in fact, the impression of him as a gentleman bootlegger at best. Telephone calls from Chicago, from Philadelphia, and from Detroit (*MS* 53, 59, 228) are related to his business activities, but do not help identify the business as such. Tom Buchanan surmises that he is "one of that bunch that hangs around Meyer Wolfshiem" (*MS* 184, 194), but Meyer Wolfshiem's explanation of how he started Gatsby in business contains no definite hint as to its nature. Since it does not implicate him in the long series of offenses that Wolfshiem himself was tried for, however, such as "grand larceny, forgery, bribery and dealing in stolen bonds" (*MS* 246), the explanation seems to support the surmise that Gatsby is a big-time bootlegger, if only by virtue of the rumors that circulate about him.

What may thus strike the reader as the author's deliberate strategy of mystifying his protagonist in the 1924 manuscript finds further elucidation in light of the subsequent correspondence between author and editor. In Perkins's detailed response to the typescript in his letter of November 20, 1924, he had three points to make about the portrayal of the protagonist: he finds Gatsby "somewhat vague"; he feels that although "his career must remain mysterious," Fitzgerald "might here and there interpolate some phrases, and possibly incidents, little touches of various kinds, that would suggest that he was in some active way mysteriously engaged" (*Life in Letters* 87); and he feels that the *en bloc* presentation of Gatsby's biography in the next-to-last chapter ought to be abandoned so that "the truth of some of his claims like 'Oxford' and his army career come out bit by bit in the course of actual narrative" (*Life in Letters* 88). In an early December 1924 letter written from Rome, Fitzgerald told Perkins that "all your criticisms are true," as well as "excellent + most helpful" (*Life in Letters* 89). This apparently also held for the charge of Gatsby's being "somewhat vague," for the author responded (somewhat cryptically) as follows: "His vagueness I can repair by *making more pointed*—this doesn't sound good but wait and see. It'll make him clear." But about three weeks later, in a more chatty letter written in a state of slight inebriation, Fitzgerald returned to Perkins's list of criticisms and as much as defended Gatsby's dimness of outline as deliberate, albeit achieved for the wrong reasons: "Strange to say my notion of Gatsby's vagueness was O.K. What you [. . .] found wanting was that: *I myself didn't know what Gatsby looked like or was engaged in* + you felt it. If I'd known + kept it from you you'd have been *too impressed with my knowledge to protest*. This is a complicated idea but I'm sure you'll understand. But I know now—and as a penalty for not having known first, in other words to make sure[,] I'm going to tell more" (*Life in Letters* 91).

In its narratological implications not unlike Hemingway's iceberg theory,[40] the answer specifies that it was not Gerlach as his model that he was uncertain about but, rather, Gatsby as a fictional character whom he had lost grasp of temporarily: "I had him for awhile then lost him + now I know I have him again." The passage as a whole similarly indicates that the author is discussing problems of character delineation, not his relation to Gerlach as an actual person. But it is also true that the actual Gerlach would seem to have continued to be somewhat enigmatic for the author and thus made it difficult for Fitzgerald to fall back on Gerlach for details in the characterization of his protagonist. For instance, as Gerlach was a small-time bootlegger at most, whatever authentic information was needed to account for Gatsby's enormous wealth must come from other sources, as it eventually did. As long as it was Gerlach's biography alone that defined the outlines of the protagonist, Fitzgerald's "notion of Gatsby's vagueness was O.K.," for—as has been pointed out—it was not Gerlach engaged in a particular business that the author was interested in as a model, but Gerlach as the dreamer of the American Dream. Whatever supplementary information was subsequently added in the galleys to account for Gatsby's money and thus help make Gatsby less vague was in fact all borrowed from other people. These additions should not, therefore, induce one to believe that Gerlach as the author's prototype had actually been a wealthy bootlegger and gangster.

Despite Fitzgerald's admission of Gatsby's vagueness in the manuscript version of the novel, there are quite a few sentences that deliberately portray Gatsby as an individual and also show what he looked like. Nick Carraway describes his neighbor as "a handsome blue-eyed man" and keeps calling him "the blue-eyed man" (*MS* 52) until Gatsby properly identifies himself. The subsequent summary of the impression Gatsby has made upon Nick continues to emphasize the stunning quality of his eyes: "He was undoubtedly one of the handsomest men I had ever seen—the dark blue eyes opening out into lashes of shining jet were arresting and unforgettable. A sort of hesitant candour opened them wide when he listened but when he spoke the hesitancy was transferred to his voice and I got a distinct impression that he was picking his words with care" (*MS* 53). In relating how Gatsby calls on him one morning in June, Nick once more comments on the striking beauty of his eyes: "He saw me looking at him and suddenly he smiled—his eyes, damp and shining like blue oil, opened up with such brilliance that it was an embarrassing brilliance" (*MS* 66).[41]

His blue eyes actually were an identifying mark of the Teutonic-featured Gerlach, as several documents show. His passport application dated November 15, 1919, for instance, whose entries are in Gerlach's own hand, lists the color of his eyes as blue (2), as does the "Registrar's Report" on Gerlach's World War II Draft Registration Card of April 26, 1942 (2). But what is remarkable is that the above description also seems to take its cue directly from that of the eleven-year-old Rudolph Miller in "Absolution." Father Schwartz, when turning around to face the boy, finds himself "staring into two enormous, staccato eyes, lit with gleaming points of cobalt light" (*Stories* 159). And later Rudolph appears as the "beautiful little boy with eyes like blue stones, and lashes that sprayed open from them like flower-petals" (*Stories* 169). Along with two further references to the beauty of his eyes (*Stories* 169, 171), these descriptions indicate an obvious continuity in the portrayal of a detail that appears to have been bound up with the German ethnic background that Fitzgerald has been shown to be interested in preserving and also point to Gerlach as the likely source for both these texts.

A second feature in the portrayal of Gatsby as striking as that of his blue eyes similarly emerges in the brief moment when Nick first meets him, before—in indirect complement to that portrayal—Fitzgerald has the butler summon Gatsby to the telephone to take a call from Chicago: "He was [no] older than me—somehow I had expected a florid and corrupulent person in his middle years—yet he was somehow not like a young man at all. There was a tremendous dignity about him, a retiscense which you could fear or respect according to your temperment but on the other hand a formality that just barely missed being absurd, that always trembled on the verge of absurdity until you found yourself wondering why you didn't laugh"[42] (*MS* 53). The formality runs to such oddity that when Gatsby "was standing in the hall, speeding his last guests" he was "bowing slightly over every lady's hand" (*MS* 59). The distinctly European and faintly aristocratic chivalrous mannerism appears ludicrous because such behavior is wholly inappropriate to the occasion and even more so to the parvenu bootlegger that Gatsby is rumored to be. The model for this almost certainly was Max von Gerlach, who was claiming a social status and aristocratic rank without having any rightful title to either. The hypercorrection in demeanor resulting from such pretension could have been intensified in Gerlach's case by the fact that he had been born in Germany, that he had had little formal education, and that for several years he had lived outside the United States, spending time in Cuba and England as well as in Germany. In the following passage in chapter 3 of the manuscript (which survives in chapter 4 of the novel only in a much revised version) the possible influence of Gerlach on the portrayal of this kind of behavior is made all but explicit by reference to what is actually termed "foreignness." At the same time the passage illustrates how, with great care and deliberation, Fitzgerald set out to develop in his protagonist the Americanness that he was about to turn into the distinguishing feature of his novel: "That faint foriegness, that ^formal^ caution ~~about every word and gesture~~ ^that enveloped ^^his^^ every word^ was less perceptible in the sunshine; ~~and~~ as he stood balancing on the dashboard of his car—he ~~I thought how~~ ^seemed very^ American ~~he was~~, after all ——. His body had ^about it^ that resourcefulness of movement ~~about it that is the particular~~ ^which^ stamp^s^ ~~of~~ all our young men~~, coming~~ ^—it is due,^ I suppose, ~~from~~^to^ the absence of heavy lifting work in youth and, even more, ~~from~~^to^ the formless grace of our nervous sporadic games" (*MS* 66). For all the American resourcefulness of movement ascribed to him, the impression of Gatsby's foreignness is retained; the author has him choke a little on the phrase "educated at Oxford," so that Nick "began to believe that there was something sinister about him after all" (*MS* 69). Gatsby's speaking with hesitancy and picking his words with great care (*MS* 53), as well as Jordan Baker's remark that Gatsby is "a terrible roughneck underneath it all" (*MS* 92), further argue for the influence of Gerlach on the author's portrayal. Gatsby's dignity and aloofness, which reassert themselves after he has proffered his spurious biography (*MS* 76), as well as the resulting isolation and reticence that are stressed throughout the text, are similarly traceable to the faint foreignness of demeanor that, according to later newspaper reports, seems to have characterized the man who had decided to cast himself as Max von Gerlach.

Fitzgerald's reaction to Perkins's response to the typescript of *The Great Gatsby* contains what seems to be yet another, even more precise reference to Gerlach specifically as a source for the portrayal of his protagonist, although again the author refrains from identifying him by name. Supporting his argument of Gatsby's vagueness, Perkins suggested that "a reader [. . .] gets an idea that Gatsby is a much older man than he is" (*Life in Letters* 87). Fitzgerald replied as follows: "It seems of almost mystical significance to me that you thot he was older—the man I had in mind, half unconsciously, *was* older (a specific individual) and evidently, without so much as a definate word, I conveyed the fact.—or rather [. . .] I conveyed it without a word that I can at present and for the life of me, trace" (*Life in Letters* 91). While the manuscript did in fact state that Gatsby, although little older than the narrator, was "not like a young man at all" (*MS* 53), the typescript that Perkins saw apparently conveyed that impression solely by indirect means. But it is true that Gerlach, the "specific individual" parenthetically referred to by Fitzgerald, actually was all of 36 years of age in the summer of 1922, a full eleven years older than the author himself and six years older than his narrator. Although never referring to him by name, Fitzgerald apparently knew the "specific individual" much better than he felt it was necessary ever to admit. Details to be cited as evidence include, of course, the familiar salutation "old sport," which Fitzgerald then decided to turn into Gatsby's defining expression.[43] Another look at such details as particulars borrowed and adapted for the purposes of a sophisticated novel has Gerlach emerge even more fully as a chief source of inspiration for a uniquely compelling fictional character. Once again the subsequent survey follows the manuscript version of *The Great Gatsby* as the document closest to the facts that the novel builds on.

One of the intriguing features in the introduction of Gatsby is the spate of rumors that circulate about him even at his own parties. While they are cited as "a tribute to the romantic speculation Gatsby inspired" (*MS* 45) and function as such, the strikingly contradictory allegations are nonetheless the very same allegations that had also been directed against Gerlach. The Report to the Bureau of Investigation in June 1917 indicates that Gerlach was indeed suspected of having been "a German spy during the war" (*MS* 45), just as Fitzgerald puts it in his manuscript. And while the charges of Gatsby's being "a nephew or a cousin of Kaiser Wilhelm's" (*GG* 28) and "a nephew to von Hindenburg" (*GG* 49) are effective speculative extensions (as is that of his having "killed a man once" [*MS* 45]), the additional charge of his having grown up in Germany again holds for Gerlach—as does the exonerating circumstance that he was in fact "in the American army during the war" (*MS* 45). The latter detail thus concludes a series of correspondences between the experiences of an actual person and those of a character in fiction altogether too strange to be found coincidental. But these experiences appear nonetheless believable and are in fact uniquely successful in sketching both the protagonist and the world in which he moves, and in doing so they furnish a perfect instance of Fitzgerald's ability and eagerness to embrace and adapt particular aspects of Gerlach's story.

For Fitzgerald, who had served in the US Army from October 1917 to February 1919 and for whom his military service continued to loom large in his imagination, it would have been natural in the early 1920s to talk with others about his wartime record, just as Nick Carraway does with Gatsby at their first meeting. It is perhaps no coincidence, therefore, that Gatsby was commissioned as first lieutenant, just as Gerlach was, and that Gatsby was discharged as major, the very rank that Gerlach, along with the nobility predicate, seems to have appropriated after the war.[44] Like Fitzgerald, however, and unlike Gatsby, Gerlach was not sent overseas. Gatsby's battle experience and his deeds of courage, needed for purposes of characterization and plot development, were evolved from other sources at hand,[45] and the particulars of the Meuse-Argonne Offensive were researched and adjusted with care so as to render them historically probable.[46] But as a person "in trouble over bootlegging," Gerlach may well have functioned as Fitzgerald's source for some of the details surrounding Gatsby's alleged activities as a bootlegger. A passage in the manuscript, for instance, reflects Gerlach's situation after his discharge in 1919. At the same time it also draws on Fitzgerald's own memory of that year, and so, while providing extenuating circumstances for a demobilized soldier's drifting into a criminal career, it also helps to explain the ambivalent feelings that the narrator is to develop toward the protagonist: "It was such wild luck that he should have run into Wolfshiem— Gatsby of all the young officers that flushed, feverish spring poured loose into New York. After losing Daisy he must have been ripe for anything and there were ~~lots of~~ ^a good many^ others beginning life over again at twenty dollars a week who would have welcomed such remunerative corruption and even found in it the vanishing stimulus of the war" (*MS* 246). As I have noted earlier, Gerlach's various jobs and activities in the United States and abroad as well as, most notably, his military service and family background were indeed singularly appropriate qualifications for a successful career as a big-time gentleman bootlegger (see "The Real Jay Gatsby" 45–83), although it is not likely that he actually attained such a status. But there is one specific detail in Gerlach's records, the American Legion tie pin that he is shown to wear in his 1919 passport application photo, that apparently inspired what is a memorable scene in Gatsby's career. It is this detail that Meyer Wolfshiem is made to stress in his eulogistic obituary, along with choosing words that in a general way fit the situation of Gerlach as well as that of Gatsby: "A young major in the army covered over with medals he got in the war. He was so poor he had to keep on wearing his uniform because he couldn't buy any regular clothes. [. . .] I raised him up out of nothing, right out of the gutter. I saw right away he was [a] fine appearing gentlemanly young man and when he told me he was an Oggsford I knew I could use him good. I got him to join up in the American Legion and he got to stand high there [. . .]" (*MS* 245). Gatsby and Gerlach (along with Fitzgerald himself), thus, shared the defining experience of war and the excitement of the veteran's return to civilian life, and the fact that Gerlach advertised his membership in the American Legion (involving a commitment on his part that was to last until the time of his death, the Legion sending a clergyman to officiate at his funeral in 1958 [see Burial Records 1]) once more points to his person as a probable source of an interesting particular.[47]

But Gerlach had never fought on a European battlefield and did not get sent to Oxford after the Armistice. He did visit the United Kingdom in 1910, however, perhaps in his capacity as manager of the Motor Car Exchange of 250 West 84th Street of New York City, for the ship's manifest lists his occupation as "machinist."[48] Given Gerlach's impulse to act as a confidence man, he could perhaps have exploited that visit along with his other social pretensions. It is a fact, after all, that in 1939 he told his last landlady that "he was a former German baron" and that "he had attended some English university," while Miss Elizabeth Mayer, in whose apartment he shot himself in the head, testified to his "military bearing" and his "Oxford accent."[49]

It is true, then, that the biography of Max von Gerlach, such as Fitzgerald came to know it, included fraudulent claims to social distinction. A spurious university connection, the self-conferred rank of major, and his pretended nobility, however helpful they may have been to Gerlach in starting and pursuing a civilian career, also made his social status a precarious one. In addition to the danger of getting into trouble as a bootlegger, these accusations could have made him behave as cautiously and strangely as Gatsby is shown to do by his author. I suggest that Fitzgerald, in his attempt to underscore the peculiar Americanness of the rags-to-riches story of his protagonist, found Gerlach's nobility pretensions anything but the right material for his purposes, just as the Catholic element of the original plan would have run counter to the idea of a novel that, according to the author's unfulfilled last-minute wishes, was to have been titled "Under the Red, White, and Blue." Accordingly, the matter is kept on the level of mere rumor, where the author knew to turn it to great effect, though. Much more is made by Fitzgerald of Gerlach's pretended rank of major, but again the author adapted the motif, slowly and effectively dispelling Nick Carraway's disbelief regarding Gatsby's military exploits rather than expose him as a braggadocio. What on the basis of available evidence must have figured lowest in the hierarchy of Gerlach's pretensions, the Oxford connection that really might have been no more than a playful attribution to begin with, seems to have been turned to greatest account in the writing of the novel. To have decided to take up and exploit this detail and have Gatsby pretend to be "an Oxford man" must rate as a sheer stroke of genius on the part of Fitzgerald.[50] It fits the character of his protagonist and the exigencies of his plot in equal measure, giving the author the opportunity to develop Gatsby's social pretension out of the very twist in the story (the delayed return from the war) that precipitates his loss of Daisy and the corruption of his dream. Moreover, the claim of being an Oxford man as it is used to structure the novel through a sequence of varying versions of the story and varying responses to these, admits a denouement that in the end does enable Gatsby to save his face, at least in the eyes of the narrator. When Nick Carraway learns about the circumstances of Gatsby's stay there and hears him say that he "can't really call [himself] an Oxford man," he has another one "of those renewals of complete faith in him" that he has experienced before (GG 100–01). Such resolution may indeed reflect the particular nature of Gerlach's various fabrications as well. The nobility presumption, above all—if it did in fact grow out of his father's official position with the German Royal Court and as an officer in the Prussian Army, alongside of actual "von Gerlachs"—would seem similarly defensible to a sympathetic witness who grants a man the right "to invent his own antecedents," as the key line reads in chapter 8 of the revised and rewritten galleys—which as such was prompted by the story of none other than Max Gerlach.

Claiming to be "an Oxford man" is made for Gatsby to be a part of his endeavor to invent what in a material metaphor is called "a golden spoon for himself" (MS 216): "I come from very wealthy people in the middle-west—all dead now. I was brought up in America but educated at Oxford because all my forefathers have been educated there for many years" (MS 69). Toward the end of the manuscript, however, in the crucial passage quoted above, Fitzgerald has the narrator use a more elevated language to assess the fabrication. Having Jay Gatsby spring "from his platonic conception of himself" and calling him "a son of God," the narrator now concludes that his family "were less than nothing to him" (MS 216). Just as the Corona dumps that Fitzgerald had been passing on his way to New York City to attend the rehearsals of his play, The Vegetable, were imaginatively transformed, first into the ash heaps of the interim title of his novel, "Among the Ash Heaps and Millionaires" (*GG*, "Appendix 2" 206) and then into the Valley of Ashes of *The Great Gatsby*, so were Max Gerlach's fabrications about himself and his past imaginatively transformed, first into Gatsby's mundane invention of a golden spoon and then into a consummate symbolic gesture that transcends its origins in the particular behavior of a real person who survives in the author's records solely as a nameless "specific individual" referred to only parenthetically and in passing.

Again such findings prove that resurrecting Gerlach and studying the details of his biography as a case history help Fitzgerald scholarship to measure the achievement of *The Great Gatsby* as myth. To critics and readers who are working solely from the printed text of the novel, on the other hand, the claim that is being made for Gerlach as an important inspiration for the portrayal of the protagonist must seem less convincing, not least because of additional source materials that have found considerable notice in Fitzgerald scholarship and directed attention away from Gerlach to persons who played a more conspicuous role in the world of the Roaring Twenties. Most of these additional materials, however, became part of the text only when the author began to revise the work according to the criticism and suggestions made by Perkins. About the middle of February 1925, "after six weeks of uninterrupted work" (*Life in Letters* 95), Fitzgerald returned the revised galleys and in a letter to Perkins specified the nature of his revisions and additions. The first two points in his list in particular concern the portrayal of his protagonist: "(1) I've brought Gatsby to life; (2) I've accounted for his money" (*Life in Letters* 96). As early as in his second letter of December 1924, he had told Perkins that for the latter point he was planning to draw on the Fuller-McGee case: "[. . .] after careful searching of the files (of a man's mind here) for the Fuller Magee case + after having had Zelda draw pictures until her fingers ache I know Gatsby better than I know my own child" (*Life in Letters* 91).

Edward M. Fuller and William F. McGee were partners in a New York brokerage firm that did business mostly by telephone and defrauded its customers by selling worthless oil securities, gambling with their funds, and squandering their money. The firm declared itself bankrupt in June 1922. The ensuing trials, four altogether, took place during the period that the Fitzgeralds were living on Long Island. The trials revealed the firm's wide scope of illegal business, as well as Fuller's far-reaching ties with prominent New York City officials, politicians, and businessmen, including William S. Silkworth, president of the Consolidated Stock Exchange, as well as Arnold Rothstein. The galley corrections of the novel, its inserts above all, demonstrate how Fitzgerald wove the particulars of the much-publicized case into the story and in doing so transformed Gatsby from the bootlegger he was rumored to be in the manuscript version into the big-time operator involved in a wide range of criminal activities in the final version of the text. Gatsby's statement, "Oh, I've been in several things [. . .], I was in the drug business and then I was in the oil business, but I'm not in either one now [. . .]" (*RRG* 76), and the telephone call from Chicago, "Young Parke's in trouble. They picked him up when he handed the bonds over the counter" (*RRG* 179), are examples from a series of inserts in which Fitzgerald "accounted for his money" and also "brought Gatsby to life." Henry Dan Piper is certainly correct in concluding that of all the author's Long Island neighbors Fuller is "the one whose outlines are most clearly discernible" in the novel (115), and it is no wonder that even before he had published his exhaustive study of Fitzgerald's use of the details of the case, Richard D. Lehan should have concluded that Fuller was the author's inspiration for Gatsby (71). However, Piper also perceived that "Fitzgerald borrowed [more] heavily from the newspaper accounts of Fuller's business affairs in creating Gatsby than he had from the details of Fuller's personality" (119). And it is true, in fact, that although the scope of Gatsby's criminal activities has become larger, the essential features of his character and demeanor as suggested by none other than the less conspicuous Gerlach had remained unchanged. The galleys and galley inserts reveal only minor adjustments. Insert A for galley 15, for instance, deletes a remark about Gatsby's "stiff dignity," but emphasizes his "formality of speech" by adding the adjective "elaborate" (*RRG* 33, 35). Insert A for galley 17 deletes "bowing slightly over every woman's hand," but substituting "ceremonious formality" as a less specific term (*RRG* 40, 41) does not alter the characterization as such.

Still, one particular galley insert is of special interest. At the beginning of what in the printed text is chapter 4, following the guest list, the author has Gatsby drive up to Nick's house to take him to lunch in New York City. The scene opens with a conversation about Gatsby's "gorgeous car" and his pride of ownership, which—with slightly more detail both in the manuscript ("It's the handsomest car in New York [. . .]." [*MS* 66]) and in the galleys—clearly reflects Gerlach's abiding professional and personal interest in high-class automobiles, even if the talk here does not center on technical matters.[51] In a way the scene would also seem to suggest that it was indeed automobiles that had brought Gerlach to Fitzgerald's door (to sell him "the most autonomous automobile on Long Island"). And it would seem to be more than coincidence that at the point where Nick's description of his ride with Gatsby actually begins, Fitzgerald decided to place the insert about Nick's disappointment "that he [Gatsby] had little to say" and that the "impression, that he was a person of some undefined consequence, had gradually faded" (*RRG* 51). This, as I have suggested above, points to and reflects a significant conclusion that Fitzgerald had arrived at in the course of writing his novel: the fact that Max von Gerlach, although he had helped Fitzgerald redefine his original plan for the novel and actually start his work, was not a suitable model to take Fitzgerald through the process of composition in its entirety. After all, even if, like Gatsby, Gerlach had at first appeared to be "a person of some undefined consequence," he had only a few years since been assessed as a man whose brain was filled with mechanics to the exclusion of everything else. However impressive his poise and fascinating his ambitions and career may have appeared to Fitzgerald in the beginning, Gerlach's biography would seem to indicate that he was no man of intellectual sophistication and ideas. Thus, while eminently suited to help lay out the ultimate plan of *The Great Gatsby* and define its momentous theme, Gerlach had his limitations as a model for the protagonist of the novel such as it had begun to develop and take shape in the course of composition.

Indeed, Fitzgerald came to see this very clearly, as he specified in two further direct references (briefly cited in the opening of my argument) to the man who had inspired his protagonist. Both were made after the publication of *The Great Gatsby* and fully agree in their final assessment of Gerlach as much as they do in—again—not mentioning him by name. Responding to incisive critical remarks made by his friend John Peale Bishop (the model of Thomas Parke D'Invilliers, the poet in *This Side of Paradise* and "author" of the epigraph to the novel), Fitzgerald wrote to him on August 9, 1925: "[Y]ou are right about Gatsby being blurred and patchy. I never at any one time saw him clear myself—for he started as one man I knew and then changed into myself—the amalgam was never complete in my mind" (*Letters* 358). In a 1927 inscription in a copy of the novel for Charles T. Scott, Fitzgerald repeated essentially the same facts: "Gatsby was never quite real to me. His original served for a good enough exterior until about the middle of the book he grew thin and I began to fill him with my own emotional life. So he's synthetic—and that's one of the flaws in this book" (*GG Documentary Volume* 27). Whatever story Gerlach—who by the time he met the Fitzgeralds had been divorced from his first wife—may have had to tell himself, the author's decision to fill the protagonist of his novel with his "own emotional life" certainly accounts for the fervor of Gatsby's feelings and the credibility of his quest. The stories of Fitzgerald's love for Ginevra King and of his courtship of Zelda Sayre, as well as Zelda's infatuation with the French aviator Edouard Jozan during the writing of the novel in France in the summer of 1924, must have intensified the presentation of the feeling of having lost "the old warm world" (*GG* 126) that pervades the novel: "One of the lost illusions that informed *The Great Gatsby*," as Bruccoli writes, "was Fitzgerald's certainty in Zelda's fidelity" (*Some Sort of Epic Grandeur* 200). In this fashion, the autobiographical element, confined so far to certain aspects in the portrait of Nick Carraway, entered into the delineation of the protagonist—after all and against all expectation. As late as April 1924, Fitzgerald had informed Perkins as follows regarding his work on the novel: "I don't know anyone who has used up so much personal experience as I have at 27. *Copperfield* and *Pendennis* were written at past 40, while *This Side of Paradise* was three books and *The B. and D.* was two. So in my new novel I'm thrown directly on purely creative work—not trashy imaginings as in my stories but the sustained imagination of a sincere yet radiant world. So I tread slowly and carefully and at times in considerable distress. This book will be a consciously artistic achievement and must depend on that as the first books did not" (*Letters* 163). In other words, after *This Side of Paradise* and *The Beautiful and Damned*, *The Great Gatsby* was not going to be another autobiographical book. Having used up, if not wasted, all of his autobiographical material, Fitzgerald concluded that the protagonist of the new novel must be the product of purely creative work. According to this early proclamation of what in the context of *Tender*

Is the Night the author was to defend as his method of composite characterization, Gatsby was to be created by combining material taken from various sources other than his own biography. This is precisely the method that he did follow in the delineation of his protagonist. One source was, as Fitzgerald told John Jamieson in 1934, perhaps "[the image of] some forgotten farm type of Minnesota that I have known and forgotten, and associated at the same moment with some sense of romance" (*Letters* 509). This protagonist, apparently, was tried out in the material from which "Absolution" came to be salvaged, rounded out, apparently, by specifics taken from Gerlach, who had appeared on the scene when the story came to be written and who, along with his ethnic background and immigrant experience, had his own Chicago and Joliet past to recommend him for a Midwestern context. In due course, perhaps even through "Absolution," the focus shifted entirely to Gerlach, who helped to transform the original plan for the novel and to develop the "new angle." But Gerlach carried the author merely to "about the middle of the book," when he was found to be able to provide no more than "a good enough exterior." At this point and for this reason, the need arose for Fitzgerald to deviate from his original plan: "I began to fill him with my own emotional life." The metaphor, to be sure, implies that what the author called the "good enough exterior" continued to function, as it did, in the rest of the novel. But the metaphor has also been shown to be only partly adequate at most. Because more than just providing an exterior, Gerlach did, in fact, do no less a thing than inspire and define the central theme of the novel. Borrowing and integrating additional details from Edward M. Fuller and the Fuller-McGee case, subsumed by Fitzgerald under the headings of "[bringing] Gatsby to life" and "account[ing] for his money," complemented the portrayal of the protagonist's circumstances even if it did not actually affect his character. The same is true of Max Fleischmann and the material evidence of his grandeur. Of the persons whom the author himself identified as sources of individual chapters—the Rumseys, the Hitchcocks, the Goddards, the Dwans, and the Swopes, as well as Robert C. Kerr, all of whom were Great Neck neighbors of the Fitzgeralds or people they knew during their residence there—only the latter made a significant contribution to the characterization of the protagonist. What Kerr told Fitzgerald about his 1907 encounter with the industrialist and yachtsman Edward Robert Gilman on Sheepshead Bay in Brooklyn and his subsequent three-and-a-half-year service as Gilman's secretary aboard his yacht resulted in the most important addition, that of the story of young Jay Gatsby and Dan Cody. But as straight rags-to-riches matter, Kerr's account proved readily compatible with the outlines of Gatsby's biography and fully consistent with the facts provided by Gerlach's life, the latter's name change and ennoblement, moreover, providing a concomitant success story motif. Further, the case can be made that Gerlach's biography offered its own provision for attaching the Dan Cody story. Gerlach also had had his rich benefactor, Cushman A. Rice, the Minnesota banker, entrepreneur, and adventurer-soldier, who had stood behind him and apparently promoted him from the time they first met in Cuba in 1909 to when Gerlach met Fitzgerald.[52] In its particular local adaptability Kerr's account also served the author well in his need to integrate the Midwestern and Great Neck materials. All things considered, then, neither Fitzgerald's own emotional life nor the additional sources, however important they finally were for the characterization of the protagonist and the impact of the novel, ever fully canceled out Gerlach and his contribution to *The Great Gatsby*. Even if he ceased to function as a model when Fitzgerald began to focus on the emotional life as the all-important quality of his character, the role Gerlach had played in creating Gatsby helped contain the autobiographical impulse and objectify the portrait of the protagonist. Fitzgerald's achievement in this regard has been well perceived by Bishop. In a second letter about *The Great Gatsby,* Bishop wrote to its author: "I can't understand your resentment of the critic's failure to perceive your countenance behind Gatsby's mask. To me it was evident enough. I haven't watched you living up to the Fitzgerald legend since 1917 for nothing. But it seems to me interesting, if at all, privately only. The point is that you have created a distinct and separate character, perhaps the first male you have ever created on the scale [word or words missing] a novel, whom you have filled, as is inevitable, with your own emotional life. But to ask people to see you in Gatsby seems to me an arrant piece of personal vanity; as an artist it should flatter you that they did not see it" (*Correspondence* 175). If Gatsby turned out to be a distinct and separate character after all, it was Gerlach who helped to make him such.

Conclusion

Zelda Fitzgerald's remarks of 1947 concerning Gerlach's role in the composition of *The Great Gatsby,* rather than being taken at face value, have had a curiously confused history of reception in Fitzgerald scholarship. Inadequately transcribed to begin with, disregarded, misinterpreted, and even misread so as to fit preconceived ideas about the novel and its genesis, not to mention belittled in their relevance, they have come to prejudice and harm scholarly investigation rather than promote our understanding of how the novel was conceived and written. At the same time they have continued to hold out the challenge of further investigation as occasional information about Gerlach happened to turn up. And it is in fact through the full range of the disparate bits and pieces of information that have been retrieved in a prolonged endeavor such as only a great work of literature would seem to warrant, that we now perceive Zelda's information about the model for Gatsby to be both true and relevant in all of its detail: "a Teutonic-featured man named von Gerlach," "a neighbor named von Gerlach or something who was said to be General Pershing's nephew and was in trouble over bootlegging." Moreover, we now see much more clearly the significance of what Zelda told Piper about Gerlach as the inspiration for her husband's novel. Max von Gerlach was a German immigrant with a captivating immigrant biography to tell. Given the degree of correspondence, for instance, between the rumors that circulate about Gatsby at his own parties and the facts and actual rumors about Max von Gerlach that have at long last been recovered and verified beyond all doubt, we now gather that Fitzgerald must have been an attentive listener as Gerlach talked about his life, relating details of his quest for identity and his story of becoming an American. In this broadening of the material basis of evidence, facts have come to light that, rather than merely substantiate previous findings, bring about a fundamental change in perspective. The need to go to great length to reexamine and then disprove the myth of Max von Gerlach as the wealthy Long Island gentleman bootlegger, a cherished myth in the popular imagination well beyond the field of literary scholarship, has cleared the way for the discovery of Gerlach's ambiguous attitude toward telling his story as the real point of interest for Fitz-

gerald and his novel. Observing Gerlach present partly fraudulent and contradictory accounts of his biography and implicitly reject and deny certain
parts of it, Fitzgerald adopted this procedure to devise similarly conflicting
accounts of Gatsby's career as circulating about, and presented by, his protagonist. Rephrasing, in successive stages of composition, a series of exonerating explanations that culminate in his narrator's reflections about Gatsby
springing "from his Platonic conception of himself" and being "a son of God"
who "must be about His Father's Business" (*GG* 77), Fitzgerald in effect used
the example of Gerlach to define the idea of the American Dream and so to
arrive at the central theme of his novel. The focus is on Gatsby as dreamer
of the dream rather than as a bootlegger set on actually trying to realize it,
the latter view a misreading helped along perhaps by seeing his model as the
gentleman bootlegger that plainly he never was. Gerlach, thus, in addition to
merely helping Fitzgerald transform the original plan for his novel, prevailed
as a source of inspiration throughout the composition of his work. This also
holds for Gerlach as an inspiration for Gatsby as a character, for while Fitzgerald did begin to fill his exterior with his own emotions, his protagonist's
demeanor as developed in the opening chapters continued to be essentially
the same. What had not been perceived earlier and what emerges only now
that a wider range of Gerlach's self-testimony has been recovered, is the impact that the Fitzgerald-Gerlach encounter has had on the narrative structure of the novel. In its persuasive strategy of withheld information, it mir-
rors Fitzgerald's very process of gradually learning ever more about Gerlach
and thus fittingly complements the author's thematic concerns.

The more complete body of information about Gerlach as an actual immigrant leads to a reconsideration of the importance of Gatsby's ethnic background. It had seemed earlier that when Fitzgerald began to draw on his own
emotional life for the portrayal of Gatsby, he had allowed the German element to recede and that therefore there was no need "to begin to read the
novel [. . .] in terms of the German ethnic background of its protagonist"
("The Real Jay Gatsby" 75). But it now emerges that the acts of rejection involved in both Gerlach's and Gatsby's denials of past and parents are actually rejections of the old world in favor of the new, as well as a necessary and
eloquent correlative of the American Dream as opted for by both Gatsby
and his model. The context of composition—Fitzgerald's concurrent expo-

sure to the counsel of Mencken, to Nietzsche, and to Ludendorff, as well as the avowed impact of Spengler—furthermore argues for the presence of the German element, if merely as an important subtext not to be ignored. As such it helps curb speculations about Gatsby's ethnic origins that proceed from the deliberate obscurity of his background as well as the insecurity of his deportment, both of which are now readily traceable to the biography of Gerlach as a German immigrant.

The much broader base of documents and data about Gerlach and the wider scope of their reflection in the novel suggest that what Fitzgerald had his narrator say about Gatsby at the very outset of his retrospective account—that he gradually "came to dominate [. . .] the story of that summer on Long Island" and that he became "the only one to leave footprints in that vacuum after all"—can also be read as the author's considered judgment of the role of Gerlach as his model in the actual course of composition of his narrative. Such a conclusion notwithstanding, my contention needs repeating that in the very act of developing its central theme from the particulars of Max von Gerlach's biography *The Great Gatsby* transcends these and all its other sources. But the study of these sources in their variousness and often incidental nature has us see how Fitzgerald's art, here as much as always, evolved from and flourished on the finely observed detail of the immediate circumstances of his life, and how such circumstances combined with what the author was learning from his uncommonly perceptive reading, to produce a work like *The Great Gatsby*.

Dinner at the Buchanans'

Eugenics and the Beginning of *The Great Gatsby*

In the density of its structure and the tight development of its plot, Fitzgerald's *The Great Gatsby* quickly moves the reader's attention from one scene to another. It appears to privilege later sections, culminating in the drawn-out epilogue with Nick Carraway's night-thoughts on the beach of Long Island Sound at the end of the final chapter. By comparison, the opening scene of the novel, Fitzgerald's description of a small dinner party at the Buchanans', would seem to command less interest. It certainly has its share of memorable phrases, from the reference to people who "played polo and were rich together" (*GG* 9) all the way to Gatsby himself, "come out to determine what share was his of our local heavens" (*GG* 20)—an imposing sequence of arresting expressions. Yet the scene pretends (as opening scenes tend to do) to be a comparatively modest array of details and facts. One does appreciate its remarkable unity as well as the clever arrangement and rearrangement of the configuration of characters: in a ballet-like sequence of pas de deux, we have all dinner guests do their twosome performances, in addition to other groupings, resulting in highly effective indirect characterization, one of the strong points of the author's narrative technique. One also notes, for instance, the seemingly playful reference to a nightingale on Daisy's lawn "come over on the Cunard or White Star Line" (*GG* 16) and a more serious bandying of the word "civilization," and the reader begins to suspect that in these instances—

as Ronald Berman puts it—"there are echoes meant to be heard" (*Fitzgerald–Wilson–Hemingway* 27). But it is only in light of what follows in the novel—and in light of ever-new critical approaches and new factual evidence—that the scene gathers in import and goes to support the conclusion that *The Great Gatsby* is in fact "inexhaustible" (Bruccoli, *New Essays* 12).

My own approach is twofold: focusing on the opening scene I shall first turn to literary history and then consider autobiographical as well as other source material. The combination of these approaches along with new material evidence will lead to a clearer view of how to figure both the genesis of *The Great Gatsby* and its meaning as a novel of ideas.

∼

Appreciation of dinner at the Buchanans' is much enhanced by viewing the scene in the context of the novel of manners. Descriptions of dinners as well as other social functions are a staple feature in novels that follow in the tradition established by Jane Austen. They are an important means of characterizing social groups as well as individuals. The procedure works best and is used to great effect in what is called the dramatic novel, notably when the rituals involved and the tacit assumptions that are made are challenged by historical development and concomitant social change.

Regardless of deliberate intertextual relatedness between these scenes, the dinner parties as described in William Dean Howells's *The Rise of Silas Lapham* (1885) and Edith Wharton's *The Age of Innocence* (1920), long since seen as set pieces, suggest themselves for comparison. Like Silas Lapham, Nick Carraway is an interloper in the world of moneyed aristocracy. In either instance, it is prospective or existing family relationships that account for the invitation. In each case, the reader's sympathy is with the interloper, who is made to feel "uncivilized" and then brings to bear his own rural and naive views on moneyed aristocracy in its sophistication. In each case, alcohol loosens the tongue of the interloper: Lapham, under the influence of too much wine and postprandial Madeira, proceeds to set an authentic account of heroic sacrifice against fabricated sacrifice as described in the popular sentimental novel of the day; Carraway, "on [his] second glass of corky but rather impressive claret" (*GG* 13–14), attacks a similar kind of inconsequential banter and suggests (albeit jokingly) a more substantial subject for discussion: "crops or something" (*GG* 14). In each case, the moneyed aristocracy proceeds to defend its position against the intruder. With similar success it also restrains and retains Newland Archer, the weak defector, in *The Age of Innocence,* while dinner conversation at the same time touches on the danger to society of "tolerating men of obscure origin and tainted wealth" (*AI* 282), just as if the debate were, in fact, about Jay Gatsby, "Mr. Nobody from Nowhere" (*GG* 101), in Tom Buchanan's estimation.

The vast conspiracy that Archer finds to be at work at the farewell dinner given for Ellen Olenska (ironically exposed as a "tribal rally around a kinswoman about to be eliminated from the tribe" [*AI* 279]), and its milder form shown to operate in the planning of the dinner at the Coreys', clearly survive in the description of dinner at the Buchanans'. Nick, after listening to Daisy's insincere protestations of ennui and sophistication, finds "an absolute smirk on her lovely face as if she had asserted her membership in a rather distinguished secret society to which she and Tom belonged" (*GG* 17). The narrator's observation at this early point in the novel foreshadows the conspirational intimacy between Daisy and her husband as described at the end of chapter 7 as well as their retreating "back into their money or their vast carelessness or whatever it was that kept them together" (*GG* 139) as envisioned by Nick near the end of the novel.

The foils of dinner in Bellingham Place and in the house of the Wellands in Old New York are helpful and even essential in having us perceive basic shortcomings in the Buchanans at what, admittedly, is a more private dinner. As with the Coreys and the Archers, there are servants, but the butler at the Buchanans' gets talked about a soon as he leaves the table. On the dinner table there are candles, but the candles get snuffed and lit again according to no plan. Dinner is disrupted by a telephone call from Myrtle Wilson, whom Jordan Baker hastens to identify for Nick as Tom's mistress, violating all rules of discretion that govern social behavior at the table of the Coreys and the Archers. As young Tom Corey informs Lapham, "Excuse me, my father doesn't talk his guests over with one another" (*SL* 185). There is an obvious hint at traditional etiquette when Jordan finds that Myrtle "might have the decency not to telephone him at dinner-time" (*GG* 16). But at the same time Jordan "leaned forward, unashamed, trying to hear" (*GG* 15), after Tom has left the table without excusing himself (as one notes), and after Daisy, who does excuse herself, has followed him, unmindful of the rule not to leave one's guests alone. These are signs and symbols of dissolution, as are the numerous references to, and signs of, restlessness, instability, and lack of purpose, best expressed, perhaps, in the notorious exchange between Jordan and Daisy: "'We ought to plan something,' yawned Miss Baker, sitting down at the table as if she were getting into bed. 'All right,' said Daisy. 'What'll we plan?' She turned to [Nick] helplessly. 'What do people plan?'" (*GG* 13).

Money, to be sure, is still available to guarantee exclusiveness. Tom Buchanan plays polo just as Reggie Chivers in *The Age of Innocence* is shown to do some fifty years earlier, "practising for the International Polo match" (*AI* 281). But the rich in Fitzgerald's novel have become rootless and have lost their sense of purpose. The remarkable stability of the family homes of the Coreys and of the aristocratic families of Old New York has disappeared. The Buchanans prefer to move about, "unrestfully" (*GG* 9), with the change of the seasons. The family and group solidarity of the Coreys and Old New York is clearly missing here. Tom and Daisy have their disagreements; Jordan is a mere hanger-on. While the Coreys and the members of the aristocratic families of Old New York all instinctively share the values as well as the morals and manners of the social group they represent and calmly take them for granted, the bond between Tom, Daisy, and Jordan seems to be just riches and aristocratic leisure class activities, as well as (on Tom's part) stridently claiming and defending traditional privileges rather than, through duty and devotion, actually earning and quietly enjoying them. Indeed, Tom Buchanan's at times desperate endeavor to justify and to defend the privileges of the very rich, to define their essence, as well as to interpret the criteria of membership, are all aspects through which Fitzgerald's rendition of the dinner scene differs significantly from those of Howells and Wharton. And the latter help us more clearly to perceive and to appreciate Fitzgerald's particular achievement in his analysis of the very rich and their image (as well as their self-image) at the beginning of the American twenties.

∽

Tom Buchanan's case starts out as an early exemplification of Fitzgerald's abiding interest in the representation of the "aging" sportsman and the latter's anxiety resulting from loss of physical strength and capability. As Nick puts it in the impressive metaphor that describes Tom's case as one of arrested development: he "would drift on forever seeking a little wistfully for the dramatic turbulence of some irrecoverable football game" (*GG* 9). Yet Fitzgerald takes great pains to have his portrait of Tom Buchanan be more than an account of a pathetic case history. Buchanan is obviously drawn as a representative of his class, as one of the people who are defined, in that felicitous phrase of the author's, as being "rich together." Such a term would not and could not have been used for the rich in the novels of Howells and Edith Wharton. Buchanan does not ever seem to have been interested in pursuing a professional career, has cultivated no work ethic, or ever felt an obligation of any sort toward society or his fellow beings. And since he has never shared in any kind of intellectual life either, Buchanan falls easy prey to the lure of the ideology of the superiority of the Nordic race. "Civilization's going to pieces," he begins his racist ranting, and then points to "*The Rise of the Coloured Empires* by this man Goddard" and its theme of the utter submersion of the white race (*GG* 19). He embraces and cultivates the tenets of Nordicism because they furnish him with a rationale to usurp and to maintain a position of leadership that, although it has come to him through inherited wealth, he can no longer claim through achievement, service, or moral excellence. The ideology of the master race simply buttresses his desperate pretensions to superiority, just as it caters to his enormous vanity.

There is something very prophetic and clairvoyant in Fitzgerald's strategy of sketching Buchanan in the image of men such as were soon to be the chief proponents of racism and the credo of the master race of Nordics. Buchanan moves his guest about "as though he were moving a checker to another square" (*GG* 13), as Nick Carraway puts it, using the very imagery that was to gain currency in describing politically motivated measures taken by totalitarian regimes throughout the century. Buchanan gives an impression of fractiousness, he is contemptuous and cruel—in words as well as in deeds—and he appears "hulking" (*GG* 13) even to his wife. He quells all protest and opposition on her part, and nonetheless (to the surprise of the narrator as well as the reader) he successfully manages to enforce and maintain solidarity and even complicity. Buchanan's history as sketched in the opening scene, thus, is basically an account of how and why the ideology of the superiority of the Nordic race entered and then came to dominate twentieth-century politics.

And to the extent that this ideology touches on the role of the wealthy in America, it also is a kind of supplement to *Civilization in the United States,* the influential assessment of current views and issues as published in 1922, whose editor, Harold Stearns, had failed to assign a specific inquiry into this topic.

∽

Why Fitzgerald in his sketch of Tom Buchanan should have succeeded so well in transcending the limitations of what might appear to be a mere pathetic case history would seem to emerge from the following survey of what can actually be recovered about the genesis and the specific sources of the opening scene of his novel. A brief summary is needed at this point of what Fitzgerald's problems were as a writer when he began the composition of *The Great Gatsby,* as well as of what his attitude was toward his material. Fitzgerald felt that when he had completed his first two novels, *This Side of Paradise* and *The Beautiful and Damned,* he had fully exhausted his store of autobiographical material and needed to turn to matter outside the realm of his own experience. An early plan for his third novel, as a consequence, specifies that the "locale will be the middle west and New York at 1885" (*GG Documentary Volume* 53). But Fitzgerald apparently found it difficult to create a sustained world that was set in the past and so decided on New York City and Long Island in the early 1920s as a new setting. Quite by chance (and under circumstances partly to be guessed at rather than described with precision), he also found a substitute for the autobiographical model that had been his mainstay in structuring his earlier novels: Max (von) Gerlach, whose interesting biography (as detailed in the preceding chapter) promised to hold viable material from which to develop both plot and theme, as well as the intricate structure that the author was after. Comparing his short story "Absolution" as evolved from the material of a lost first draft of the third novel and the known facts of Max Gerlach's biography, we discover a remarkable consistency in the development of the protagonist. Both Rudolph Miller, in the story, and Max Gerlach, the actual person, represent the immigrant; both Miller and Gerlach have a specifically German background; both Miller's and Gerlach's lives are characterized by dreams and social aspirations fostered by immigrant experience; and both Miller and Gerlach actually change their names as a consequence of their dreams and social aspirations. All these traits are to be found also in James Gatz, whose very name is a distinct immigrant marker and a German one at that. Given these premises, it is obvious that when Fitzgerald began his composition he had a very clear conception of what the protagonist of the novel as well as the actual story was to be like: the protagonist was to have an immigrant background, and the story was to be that of an immigrant experience in the United States. These facts also hold the key to any assessment of Tom Buchanan as the major antagonist. A look at the materials that Fitzgerald worked from confirms that, before anything else, Buchanan as a character was constructed and developed in direct response not simply to Gatsby's money as new money, but also to Gatsby's immigrant background as well.

∼

Unlike the meeting between Gatsby and Daisy (in chapter 5), as well as the murder of Gatsby (in chapter 8) and the funeral scene (in chapter 9), dinner at the Buchanans' is not among the sections of the novel designated by the author as an "invention." Fitzgerald's listing of the sources of the individual chapters of *The Great Gatsby* in a copy of André Malraux's *Man's Hope* (1938) as preserved in the Fitzgerald Papers at Princeton University provides the following brief notation for chapter 1: "Glamor of Rumsies + Hitchcoks" (*GG Documentary Volume* 55). What seems mere general information relating to the setting of the novel turns out to be more specific in light of a May 1923 entry in Fitzgerald's *Ledger* that reads: "Met Mrs Rumsey + Tommy Hitchcock + went to parties there" (*Ledger* 177). Another entry, for November of the same year, reads: "More Rumsey parties" (*Ledger* 178). The names of both Rumsey and Hitchcock do stand out among those of the wealthy and famous residents of Long Island during the twenties. It is not at all difficult to come up with general biographical information about them, but it is the assessment of such information for the genesis of *The Great Gatsby* that would seem to need more attention than it has been given.

The "Rumsies" were Charles Cary Rumsey and his wife Mary. Charles Rumsey was born in 1879 in Buffalo, the son of a locally prominent businessman. He attended Harvard, studied sculpture in Paris and in Boston, and in 1906 set up a studio in New York City to become a successful sculptor, specializing in equestrian figures. Also a lover of horses and eventually a world-class polo champion, he met his future wife, an expert horsewoman herself, at the Meadowbrook Polo Club in Old Westbury on Long Island in 1906. They were married in 1910, had three children, and lived on their Wheatley Hills estate in Brookville, just north of Old Westbury, "out of reach of the everyday running of the Long Islanders," as Mary Rumsey once put it in a letter to her friend and neighbor Willard Straight.[1] Charles Rumsey was killed in an automobile accident on the Jericho Turnpike on September 21, 1922, a month before the Fitzgeralds rented their house in Great Neck. The 1923 Belcher Hyde Real Estate Map of Nassau County is quite up to date in listing the Rumsey property on Wheatley Road as belonging to *"Mrs.* C. C. Rumsey," and Fitzgerald's *Ledger* entry of May 1923 also specifies that it was *Mrs.* Rumsey whom he had met. Recently widowed and of an entirely different social background from that of Fitzgerald's flamboyant protagonist, Mrs. Rumsey, as well as her neighbors and friends the Hitchcocks, would have entertained and given parties quite unlike those of Gatsby's as described in chapter 3 of the novel, for which the author's list of sources consequently provides a different set of names: "Goddards. Dwanns [.] Swopes" (*GG Documentary Volume* 55). Mrs. Rumsey's hospitality along with that of the Hitchcocks, therefore, would have afforded Fitzgerald more than just a glimpse of how old money as opposed to new money was shaping their lifestyle, as well as what their particular preoccupations and opinions were. Further references in his *Ledger* throughout the twenties to both Hitchcock (181, 182) and Mary Rumsey (181, 184) and an entry about Mary Rumsey's death in 1934 (189), along with a somewhat cryptic 1930s item in his notebook about her role as an exemplary aristocrat (*Notebooks* 296, item 1732), would seem to indicate that he felt drawn to them.

Mrs. C. C. Rumsey was none other than Mary Harriman, daughter of the late E. H. Harriman, the well-known railroad czar and one of the richest men in the nation (so rich, in fact, that quite naturally the Harrimans, along with the Goulds and the Hills, figured in the short list of the wealthiest Americans imputed to Fitzgerald by Edmund Wilson in his "Imaginary Conversations" of 1924). Born in 1881, Mary Harriman attended Barnard College (class of 1905), majoring in sociology and biology and showing such interest in what was called the new "science of eugenics" that she was nicknamed "Eugenia" by her classmates ("Mrs. Rumsey Dies" 1). As part of her

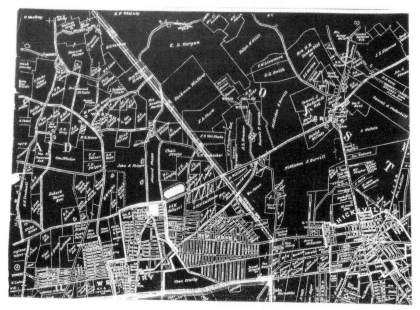

15. Old Westbury Estates, detail from 1923 Belcher Hyde *Real Estate Reference Map of Nassau County, Long Island.* Courtesy of Long Island Studies Institute, Hofstra University.

undergraduate studies, she enrolled in a biology summer course at the Carnegie Institution's recently established Station for Experimental Evolution at Cold Spring Harbor on the north shore of Long Island. A few years later, Dr. Charles Davenport, head of the installation, began to look for funding to transform the more general research on heredity that he had been doing into "specific ethnic and racial investigation" (Black 44). Davenport at this point recalled his student Mary Harriman, who then helped him establish contact with her mother and worked to win the latter over to the cause of eugenics. In 1910, "with the encouragement of the American Genetics Association" (Campbell 42), Mary Williamson Harriman, the mother, by then sole heir to the immense Harriman fortune, set up the Eugenics Record Office at Cold Spring Harbor and henceforth continued to be involved in its operation. This "gave her the sense that she was not only funding a eugenic institution, but micromanaging the control center for the future of humanity," as a historian puts it (Black 48). Bulletin #1 of the Eugenics Record Office, published in 1911, was titled *Heredity of Feeble-Mindedness,* and the author of this seminal study that documents the shift in research toward ethnic and racial concerns was a psychologist named Henry H. Goddard.[2] By 1918, the total of Mrs. Harriman's eugenic patronage had amounted to more than half a million dollars. It is safe to say that without the massive support of the Harrimans in terms of funds and property, and the example that they set to other wealthy people, the eugenics movement would never have played the role that it did in America as well as worldwide. Mrs. C. C. Rumsey, the daughter, continued her own activities on behalf of the cause, which culminated in her service on the General Committee that organized the Second International Congress of Eugenics in New York City in 1921. In 1923, the year in which Fitzgerald was to meet her, she became a member of the Advisory Council of the American Eugenics Society, a position she was to hold until her death in 1934, as a result of injuries received in a riding accident.

The "Hitchcoks" (the other name in Fitzgerald's coupling of sources for chapter 1) were Thomas Hitchcock Jr., the famous polo player who is often cited as the major source of Fitzgerald's Tom Buchanan, as well as his parents, Major Thomas Hitchcock Sr. and his wife Loulie. Thomas (Tommy) Hitchcock Jr. was born in 1900 and grew up at his wealthy parents' winter home in Aiken, South Carolina, and on their Old Westbury estate of Broad Hollow Farm on Long Island. He was trained from youth to become a world-class polo player and began to achieve ten-goal ratings, the highest ratings possible, from 1922 onward. "A puissant man standing six feet tall and weighing 190 pounds," as a writer describes him in a recent biographical sketch (Bryce), he impressed Fitzgerald not only as a prominent sportsman, but also through his courageous service as a pilot in World War I and a spectacular escape from German imprisonment to return to fighting. After the war he attended Harvard from 1919 to 1922, spending the 1920–1921 academic year at Oxford. Still unmarried in the early twenties (he was to wed Margaret Mellon Laughlin, heiress to the Mellon fortune, in 1928), Tommy was spending much time on Broad Hollow Farm, where his father, formerly a ten-goal player, too, trained all his polo ponies. His mother, an accomplished player herself, taught and coached him with great success, along with many Old Westbury neighbors. The large estate had its own polo course, and while in those days "when polo was as popular as basketball or football" are today (Bryce) there were other public and private courses on Long Island, as well as numerous tournaments where Tommy Hitchcock and Charles Rumsey were seeing much of each other, the proximity of the two estates, a little over two miles of what were then rural roads, suggests that they also trained together at the Hitchcocks'. In 1921, both men were serving on the US team at the first post-war International at Hurlingham in England, and in August and September 1922 they played, although on different teams, in the tournament for the Herbert Memorial Trophy and in the US Open in Rumson, New Jersey. There also exists tangible testimony to the friendship between the two men and their families in the bronze statue of a horse named "Good and Plenty" that Rumsey modeled expressly for Tommy Hitchcock.[3]

In addition to the above information, all that was needed for an attempt to reconstruct the events that went into the making of Fitzgerald's description of dinner at the Buchanans' was a current road map of Long Island superimposed on the 1923 Belcher Hyde map of the area, along with the help of a well-informed local resident who shared information about how to gain access to the fenced-in (and apparently condemned) former Hitchcock property. Taking the most likely route from 6 Gateway Drive, the author's erstwhile residence in Great Neck, it is an eight-mile drive, for the most part along the Jericho Turnpike, to Cambridge Avenue, to the point where what seems to have been an unnamed road in 1923, and what is now Hitchcock Lane, turns north. Fitzgerald would have gone up that lane for less than half a mile along the west side of the 97-acre Hitchcock property and then turned right into the gateway of Broad Hollow Farm to find the Hitchcock mansion on his immediate right. What he would have found is a building described in the authoritative *Long Island Country Houses and Their Architects* as "Colonial revival, white, and rambling," the two-story walls covered with white shingles. According to the authors, Robert B. MacKay et al., it is "a 17th-century house around which later additions were made" (226), eventually to create a 42-room mansion. Even in its 2005 dilapidated state and general inaccessibility, one could make out a large porch across the rear side of the building, facing south and looking out on an overgrown garden and the wide expanse of a green field gently sloping toward the polo grounds, as well as screens of trees and undergrowth effectively hiding the slightly sunken Jericho Turnpike beyond. A later check on Google Earth showed the large oval of what had been an eight-and-a-half furlong race track still clearly visible from above. The surprise comes when one turns around and discovers a detail not mentioned in MacKay's volume. At a distance of a couple of hundred yards from the now inaccessible porticoed entrance to the mansion there stands an enormous oversized barn-like building that turns out to be (or to have been) immense stables and paddocks in almost pristine condition, ready to accommodate a string of polo horses of perhaps forty or more, the building, no doubt, where the Hitchcock polo ponies were, in fact, stabled.

This scene, as encountered in 2005, preserved not only the splendor of Long Island's past as "the nation's cradle of polo" ("Farm Sold"), but also important details of what was basic to the making of Fitzgerald's opening chapter. Locating the Hitchcock and the Rumsey estates on the map, discovering their proximity to each other and their relative proximity to Fitzgerald's residence in Great Neck as well as to Cold Spring Harbor, finding evidence of the friendship between the Rumseys and the Hitchcocks, establishing the identity of Mrs. C. C. Rumsey as that of Mary Harriman, and finding out about her commitment to the cause of eugenics and her involvement in the setting up of the Eugenics Record Office in Cold Spring Harbor—all these provide hints as to how Fitzgerald proceeded in constructing the opening scene of his novel.

However interesting and informative the author's appropriation of specific details may be for what it tells us about the novel and the writer, the true impact of Fitzgerald's encounter with what he calls the "Glamor of Rumsies + Hitchcoks" is of a more general nature. It concerns three distinct but closely related features that were to determine the composition of the opening scene and to have a profound effect on the novel as a whole: (1) the very rich, the possessors of old money; (2) the equestrian culture of Long Island; and (3) eugenics and the ideology of the racial superiority of Nordics.

Neither Fitzgerald's concern with the rich nor actual encounters with members of the moneyed aristocracy, male or female, were in any way new to the author when he arrived on Long Island in 1922. But the point needs to be made that in terms of the distribution of wealth generally, and certainly on Long Island itself, the mansions of the Old Westbury estates were indeed housing the richest of the rich with "blue-book names like Whitney,

16. Overgrown entrance to Tommy Hitchcock residence, Broad Hollow Farm, Old Westbury, Long Island, 2005. Author photo.

17. Stables at Broad Hollow Farm, Old Westbury, Long Island, 2005. Author photo.

Post, Morgan and Phipps" ("Farm Sold")—and old money rather than new. The East Egg of *The Great Gatsby* is located on Manhasset Bay, to be sure, as dictated by the needs of the plot and the novel's unique topography, but its components and distinguishing features are chiefly those of the neighborhood of "large homes and spacious lots" ("Farm Sold") where the Hitchcocks and the Rumseys chose to live.

For the Hitchcocks, as well as many other families, this choice was determined by the equestrian culture sustained in this vicinity. The names of the neighborhood figured on the national polo team as much as in the social register: Bird, von Stade, Wanamaker, and Winthrop, for instance, in addition to those mentioned previously. The sport was "prohibitively expensive" (Aldrich 128), since large grounds were required for practice. Particularly with the introduction of thoroughbred stock, promoted above all by William Collins Whitney, and with the need for more than one horse per game in what became an ever-faster sport, "polo slipped out of reach of the moderately well-to-do and into the hands of the very rich" (Aldrich 130). For them, horsemanship figured naturally and prominently in their lives. For the

Rumseys (as has been shown) horses were involved in all major phases and turning points in their biographies, right down to the riding accident that was the cause of Mary Rumsey's death in 1934. Tommy Hitchcock's mother, who died the same year, and Edith May Rudolph, second wife to William Collins Whitney, who died in 1899, were also victims of riding accidents. Stables, paddocks, and polo ponies, rather than a garage and showy automobiles, were features of Old Westbury well into the 1920s. In fact, the opposition between time-honored equestrian culture and the incipient automotive culture of the early twenties served Fitzgerald well to juxtapose old money and new money and to illustrate the antagonism between Buchanan and Gatsby as their respective representatives. Indeed, Buchanan's remarks to Gatsby, in chapter 7, about making garages out of stables and making a stable out of a garage, as he himself did, appear especially pertinent in view of Old Westbury as perceived by Fitzgerald through privileged glimpses of its life and ways in the company of the Hitchcocks and the Rumseys as constituent members of its horse-owning aristocracy. To emphasize the importance of this aspect for the construction of Buchanan and the portrayal of the very rich, there is a curious scene in chapter 6 that elaborates the clash of the two cultures and its implications. Fitzgerald has Buchanan visit Gatsby's house for the first time on a Sunday morning, and Nick Carraway reports the incident as follows: "[. . .] somebody brought Tom Buchanan in for a drink. [. . .] They were a party of three on horseback —Tom and a man named Sloane and a pretty woman in a brown riding habit who had been there previously." Gatsby is "delighted" that they have "dropped in" and eager to serve them and engage them in conversation:

> "Did you have a nice ride?"
> "Very good roads around here."
> "I suppose the automobiles——"
> "Yeah." (*GG* 79)

The party remain standoffish, even haughty, until the woman, on the strength of two highballs, suggests to Gatsby that they "all come over to [his] next party" and then proceeds to invite Gatsby in turn to come along to a supper party of her own. Unaware that he is not actually wanted, his voluble response is made to set him off further from the people on horseback: "I haven't got a horse [. . .]. I used to ride in the army but I've never bought a horse. I'll have to follow you in my car. Excuse me for just a minute" (*GG* 80). The juxtaposition of old money with its equestrian culture and new money with its showy automotive display is epitomized (even emblematized) by the author in the totally incongruous, almost Chaplinesque image he invokes of a party that is made up of three people on horseback and one man in a car moving along a Nassau County country road. The episode ends, however, when "Gatsby with hat and light overcoat in hand came out the front door" (*GG* 81), just as, at the insistence of Mr. Sloane, his visitors have trotted down the drive. Fitzgerald effectively cut off and foreshortened the scene. In its original continuation he had been needlessly explicit by having Gatsby, in his emulation of the rich who have just snubbed him, consider "getting a horse" himself: "'I'd like to ride tonight,' he said thoughtfully, 'I could telephone a barn in New York and have one sent out to me in a big van'" (*MS* 100)—totally unaware, of course, that such a measure will never take him closer to East Egg, that his money will not help him buy a place in society any more than it will help him buy back the past. It is true that riding a horse while serving as an officer had helped to make social disadvantage disappear, just as wearing a uniform had done as long as the war lasted. But that experience proved to be solely a temporary one, for Gatsby as much as it had for Fitzgerald himself.[4]

Going by Fitzgerald's general reliance in his composition on "the Long Island atmosphere that [he] had familiarly breathed," as he put it ("My Lost City" 112), there is every reason to believe that the "pretty woman in a brown riding habit, who had been there previously" and is apparently unmarried but still in a position to decide to invite Gatsby to her supper party, is in fact based on Mary Harriman Rumsey and that this is a true Fitzgeraldian tribute to her as a Long Island socialite and neighbor in 1923.[5] But whether she actually made it into the novel as a person is of little concern in view of the prominent presence of the ideas for which she stood. Beyond all doubt, it is largely Mary Harriman Rumsey who is responsible for the role of the ideology of eugenics as the third and most important component in the alliance of forces that oppose the protagonist even before he is allowed to come on stage in person. And it is this third component in the construction of Tom Buchanan that is most clearly conceived in response to Gatsby as a person with an immigrant background and to his story as that of an immigrant experience.

Given Fitzgerald's prior exposure to, and obvious interest in, eugenic thinking as early as during his Princeton years, it is not unlikely that the theory and its implications should have become a topic of conversation between the author and his hostess on Long Island. In her investigation of Fitzgerald's undergraduate years, Anne Margaret Daniel points to lectures by the sociologist E. A. Ross on "The Comparative Value of Races" and by Edwin Grant Conklin, professor of embryology, on "Heredity and Eugenics" that may have been the cause of the author's discussion of the superior characteristics of blond men in *This Side of Paradise*. Conklin was to be one of the few eminent faculty members during Hibben's presidency to be mentioned by name in Fitzgerald's 1927 sketch, "Princeton" (10). Daniel also notes that Fitzgerald sent an inscribed copy of Samuel J. Holmes's *The Trend of the Race: A Study of the Present Tendencies in the Biological Development of Mankind* to Judge Sayre, his father-in-law, confiding that he found it "most interesting" (Daniel 17). Perhaps the strongest piece of evidence for Fitzgerald's familiarity with eugenics is a song that he wrote for the Triangle Club production *Fie! Fie! Fi-Fi!* in 1914, expressly titled "Love or Eugenics." The text, innocuous as it seems in its reference to a "prophylactic dame" (*Poems* 19), was written to appeal to wider collegiate audiences. It thus presupposes a general familiarity with the movement and a topical interest in it, as much as it indicates the author's own familiarity with the subject as a matter of current debate. This is not surprising in view of the fact that a book such as William E. Castle's *Genetics and Eugenics* of 1916 could quickly become a popular textbook in this field and that "the large majority of American colleges and universities [. . .] offered well-attended courses in eugenics, or genetics courses that incorporated eugenic material" (Kevles 69). The very term *eugenics* began to be widely used in public discourse. In fact, so prevalent and urgent were discussions of eugenics and the related issues of race, immigration, Native Americanism, and civilization that Ronald Berman, in his exhaustive survey of such "contexts" of Fitzgerald's novel, arrived at the conclusion that "Tom Buchanan would not have been perceived as a crank in the period from 1921 to 1923" (*"The Great Gatsby" and Modern Times* 24). As early as 1917, Fitzgerald had begun to note the larger implications of such debates when, in his review of Shane Leslie's *The Celt and the World* in the *Nassau Literary Magazine,* he returned to Leslie's foreword in *The End of a Chapter* (1916) to cite a sentence about "the suicide of the Aryan race."[6] Quoting most of the above evidence and additionally pointing to the young author's professed familiarity with the work of Charles Darwin and with Ernst Haeckel's biogenetic law, Bert Bender argues that eventually "the principles of eugenics, accidental heredity, and sexual selection [will] flow together as the prevailing undercurrent in most of Fitzgerald's work before and after *The Great Gatsby*" (400).[7]

Given, on the one hand, Henry Goddard's prominence in the eugenics movement, his connection with Cold Spring Harbor, and his continued contact with Charles Davenport—as well as the fact that from 1917 onward his research on feeblemindedness gained notice in connection with the question of immigration restriction (see Kevles 82) and the development of relevant intelligence tests—and given, on the other hand, Fitzgerald's tendency to stay close to personal experience in constructing the opening scene of his novel, the use of Goddard's name seems to have been deliberate rather than mistaken. Fitzgerald appears to have known, and expected his readers to know, what he was about in his references. "This man Goddard," cited by Buchanan as the author of *The Rise of the Coloured Empires,* is neither (as has been assumed by respectable critics and editors) a reference to Lothrop Stoddard, the Scribner author of *The Rising Tide of Color,* nor is it (as one scholar assumes) pseudonymous (Slater 54). Rather, the reference is to Dr. Henry H. Goddard, who was probably the most important person, certainly from the point of view of the Cold Spring Harbor installation, to further the cause of eugenics by lending it academic respectability. As Director of Research at the Vineland Training School for Backward and Feeble-Minded Children at Vineland, New Jersey, the first known laboratory to study mental retardation, Goddard was able to furnish statistical data on humans rather than merely on animals and so to help Davenport define the new focus of the Eugenics Record Office. Goddard also translated the Binet intelligence test from the French, which then became the basis of the American I.Q. test. And he invented the term *moron* for mentally retarded people, a word that was quick to enter the general vocabulary. Fitzgerald was using it as early as in "The Offshore Pirate" (278), written toward the end of 1919, and in the last chapter of *The Beautiful and Damned* (342), written in 1921. But most important perhaps in terms of Goddard's impact is the fact that in 1913 he started his intelligence testing program for immigrants on Ellis Island. This latter activity—along with other work of his—strongly supported popular and political agitation on behalf of what became the Immigration Act of 1924, also know as the National Origins Act because it restricted the numbers of immigrants from so-called "undesirable" racial groups. Alan Margolies has called attention to Goddard's various activities and speculated about "when Fitzgerald first knew of these theories and how much, if any, of Stoddard and Goddard he read" (82). In view of the circumstances of Fitzgerald's life at the time and, moreover, of his particular interest in eugenics in its frequently invoked implications for the history of civilizations, he certainly would have known about Goddard the scientist and the significance of his efforts as much as, at the same time, Fitzgerald would have known about such popular studies as Madison Grant's *The Passing of a Great Race* (1916) as well as Lothrop Stoddard's *The Rising Tide of Color Against White World-Supremacy* (1920) and *The Revolt Against Civilization: The Menace of the Under-Man* (1922). These latter works, no doubt, helped Fitzgerald to devise his own title, *The Rise of the Coloured Empires,* as it is used in his novel. This title was fetching enough to have caught the attention of someone like Tom Buchanan, and compelling enough, moreover, in Buchanan's emotional evocation of it, to trigger and to strengthen (all evidence, internal as well as external, to the contrary notwithstanding) what Michael Knowlin describes as "the increasingly commonplace critical assumption that Gatsby is not quite 'white'" (70). It is indeed a measure of the fervor of Buchanan's racism compounded with the rage of his jealousy that for him—in the "confusion of a simple mind" (*GG* 97), seeing "himself standing alone on the last barrier of civilization" and invoking the specter of "intermarriage between black and white"—Gatsby instinctively figures, not merely as Mr. Nobody from Nowhere, but as a member of the "undesirable" races as well—Jordan Baker's murmured protest, "We're all white here" (*GG* 101), quietly underlining the extent of Buchanan's eugenic delusion. The scene echoes and simultaneously elucidates the subtle hint at racial exclusion that occurs as early as in the opening dinner scene where Fitzgerald has Buchanan discourse on *The Rise of the Coloured Empires:* "'The idea is that we're Nordics. I am and you are and you are and——' after an infinitesimal hesitation he included Daisy with a slight nod and she winked at me again, '——and we've produced all the things that go to make civilization——oh, science and art and all that. Do you see?'" (*GG* 14).

"There was something pathetic in his concentration as if his complacency, more acute than of old, was not enough to him any more," Fitzgerald has the narrator conclude. The incident serves the author well to demonstrate how eugenics and the ideology of Nordicism are taking hold among the moneyed aristocracy, as well as to what extent thinking along eugenic lines is becoming a matter of course for its members—so much so, in fact, that it either blurs their perception of reality (seeing the other as non-Nordic, even colored) or serves them as an instrument to humiliate and inflict pain (suggesting that the other may be deficient in his or her Nordic traits). Either interpretation is a possibility, for the novel as much as for life in the twenties, as Fitzgerald—who prided himself on his familiarity with the Long Island atmosphere that he had breathed for a year and a half and that he then set out to materialize in his fiction—must have known.

The three forces that have been considered and that the protagonist of Fitzgerald's novel will be up against form an alliance in the truest sense of the word: the moneyed aristocracy sustained the equestrian culture and, in turn, derived much benefit and enjoyment from it; and to justify, to buttress, and to defend its aristocratic pretensions, it eagerly embraced the teachings of eugenics, which movement in turn was also nourished by their wealth. To which another link needs to be added: it is said that Mary Williamson Harriman was won over so easily to the cause of eugenics simply because she knew all about breeding and that "both her husband's and her father's interest in breeding racehorses had suggested to her that the laws of heredity might also be used for the amelioration of man" (Kevles 54). It is noteworthy in this context that in its beginnings the eugenics movement actually started to work through the American Breeders Association as founded in 1903. The *American Breeders Magazine*, launched in 1910, eventually became the *Journal of Heredity*, the policy of which is evident in such articles as "Immigration Restriction and World Eugenics," published in 1919 (see Black 188). And it is noteworthy, too, that many of the wealthy polo-playing Old Westbury estate owners, following in the wake of William Collins Whitney's pioneering work, were actively and successfully engaged in the breeding of thoroughbred horses.

This alliance of forces in its outspoken and strident campaign of the early twenties on behalf of what became the Immigration Act of 1924 would seem to hold a final key to the construction of Tom Buchanan as the antagonist of Jay Gatsby. In opposing immigration generally, but particularly in making "the restriction of immigration from Eastern and Southern Europe" a "cardinal point of the American Eugenics program" (Kevles 95) as laid down in a printed *Eugenics Catechism* (Kevles 325 n34), eugenicists such as Goddard and Davenport implicitly and even explicitly made reference to the cherished icon of the Statue of Liberty in its symbolic meaning.[8] In view of the statue's imposing size and projected position in New York harbor, Frédéric Auguste Bartholdi, its sculptor, had begun his work with a famous model in mind: the Colossus of Rhodes, symbol of the Greek and Roman era, and one of the Seven Wonders of the World. In her sonnet written in 1883 to help raise money for the construction of the pedestal, the American poet Emma Lazarus thus referred to the Statue of Liberty as "The *New* Colossus." At the same time her text, taking its cue from the prospective visual impact of the towering figure on Bedloe's Island, transformed what had been intended as a symbol of enlightenment into a symbol of welcome to immigrants arriving from Europe. "Mother of Exiles" thus is a further name that she chose, and the closing lines of her sonnet now convey a welcome to immigrants as much as they hold out a promise of freedom. Eventually, these lines were carved on its base to become a permanent part of the statue. The poem in its entirety, on the other hand, soon made its way into schoolbooks throughout the United States, thus providing the largest audience possible for what were to be its most famous words: "Give me your tired, your poor, / Your huddled masses yearning to breathe free." These words can be said to define the idea of America and its image in Europe in the nineteenth and at the beginning of the twentieth centuries, and it is these very words that were coming under attack when in the early twenties eugenicists increased their endeavor to curb immigration. The noble message, thus, was being rendered obsolete, and as a result the statue came to be viewed as warding off rather than greeting the immigrant. While all of America could follow the heated debate about immigration restriction in the papers, Fitzgerald himself, living in the very heartland of the eugenics movement and attending the parties hosted by one of its most prominent proponents, could hardly have avoided exposure to that movement's more radical view of the matter. I suggest that as a consequence of the then-current debate the author set out to construct Tom Buchanan with "The New Colossus" in mind and proceeded to turn his antagonist into a deliberate counter-image of the Statue of Liberty. In Fitzgerald's rendition in the opening of *The Great Gatsby,* thus, the imposing female, "a mighty woman with a torch," lifting "her lamp beside the golden door," is replaced by a "hulking" male, a "sturdy, straw haired man of thirty with a rather hard mouth and a supercilious manner [. . .] a cruel body," conveying an "impression of fractiousness" and of "paternal contempt" (*GG* 9). The same kind of substitution occurs for both the text as well as the message associated with the statue: it occurs for the book that the figure clasps in its hand, and it occurs for the lines of welcome from Lazarus's poem that are engraved on its base. The new book, the substitution, is none other than "*The Rise of the Coloured Empires* by this man Goddard," and the new text is Goddard's outright denouncement of immigration that utterly perverts and desecrates the message of the original text. Always aware of the importance of gesture (as D. G. Kehl has shown[9]), Fitzgerald deliberately appears to be drawing on Emma Lazarus's reference to "the brazen giant of Greek fame / With conquering limbs astride from land to land" as he presents to the reader what will be his very first impression of the brawny Tom Buchanan—a man "in riding clothes [. . .] standing with his legs apart on the front porch" of his "cheerful red and white Georgian Colonial mansion" (*GG* 9). Buchanan, thus, is figured as a throwback to the Old Colossus as opposed to the "New," and the indications are that his is the type that will prevail. It also emerges now that in his eugenic stance Buchanan is constructed and presented first and foremost as the antagonist of Gatsby as a person with a recognizable immigrant background rather than any other of his defining characteristics. By presenting the antagonist first, dressing him in riding clothes, having him act as the overbearing host of the opening dinner party, and having the reader enter the world of the novel, as it were, with a view of Buchanan as a brazen Colossus, Fitzgerald provides an answer to a question to be asked only at the end of the opening chapter: What share will be Gatsby's of the local heavens of Long Island? The answer is:—none.

Fitzgerald himself was much taken with the success of his portrait of Buchanan as Gatsby's antagonist: "I suppose he's the best character I've ever done," he told Perkins in December 1924 while Fitzgerald was busy revising the novel. "I think he and the brother in 'Salt' + Hurstwood in 'Sister Carrie' are the three best characters in American fiction in the last twenty years, perhaps and perhaps not" (*Life in Letters* 91). And, faced with Perkins's criticism of the supposed vagueness of Gatsby as the actual protagonist, Fitzgerald did, in fact, briefly entertain the idea "to let him go + have Tom Buchanan dominate the book." Even though Fitzgerald soon realized that "Gatsby sticks in my heart," as he put it, the thought he gave to Buchanan as a possible protagonist not merely elevates the character in his portrayal and potential, but also identifies Nordicism and eugenics as important indigenous matter for the great American novel he was in the process of creating.

A final remark seems in order apropos of Fitzgerald and eugenics: In constructing Tom Buchanan in the image of the brazen Colossus and by endowing him with an overtly racist text that proclaims the ideology of the superiority of the Nordic race, Fitzgerald (his high opinion of the success of his portrayal notwithstanding) frankly disowned him as a character and thus apparently managed to exorcize the ghost of possible earlier sympathies with the movement. In fact, there is no ambiguity whatsoever about a statement of his that occurs in his review in the *New York Evening Post* of Thomas Boyd's novel *Through the Wheat*: "No one has a greater contempt," he wrote, "than I have for the recent hysteria about the Nordic theory [. . .]" (*FSF in His Own Time* 143). As it happens, the review was published at the end of May 1923, at the very moment that Fitzgerald composed his account of dinner at the Buchanans' as the actual beginning of *The Great Gatsby*. But while the review contributes to absolve the author from any charge of blind partisanship with eugenicism, it simultaneously provides further proof of the pervasive presence of the debate over ethnic and racial issues in the world that attended the writing and nourished the texture of Fitzgerald's novel.

The Great Gatsby

A View from Kant's Window—Transatlantic Crosscurrents

"There was nothing to look at from under the tree except Gatsby's enormous house so I stared at it, like Kant at his church steeple, for half an hour" (*GG* 69). Nick Carraway's reference to the German philosopher Immanuel Kant (1724–1804) appears to be the most extraneous as well as the most arcane among the many references to actual persons, places, and incidents that give resonance to the text of *The Great Gatsby*. It concerns an interesting detail in the life of this great man, the peculiarities of whose biography have often served to satisfy the curiosity of those who were unable to read and to understand his writings. His books and his arguments were difficult to follow, because he wrote for fellow philosophers rather than for the general reader and thus did not bother to provide examples for his theories. His contemporary biographers, Ludwig Ernst Borowski, Reinhold Bernhard Jachmann, and Ehregott Andreas Christoph Wasianski, in addition to describing other idiosyncrasies in the habits of the eccentric metaphysician, all touch on his domestic life in his small house located at No. 2 Prinzessinstrasse in the city of Königsberg in East Prussia. It is Wasianski to whom the account of Kant and his steeple in all its detail must be credited. According to his testimony, Kant would sit down at his desk, a simple table, about six in the evening, and read until dusk. He would then take his station, in winter as well as summer, at the stove, from where through the window, his view passing along the north wing of the old city castle, he could see the steeple of the Löbenichtsche Kirche, the Löbenicht parish church. It was this steeple that "he would look at while he was thinking,—or actually, his eyes came to rest on it. Words never failed him to express how beneficent its distance was to his eyes. Through its daily observation in the twilight his eyes may have gotten used to it."[1] The detail, verifiable by means of additional information and documentation, became so much part of the lore surrounding the man that, even though there are biographies and critical studies that do not mention it, F. Scott Fitzgerald is likely to have encountered it as early as his Princeton days. It is known that his interest in philosophy goes back that far and that he received excellent grades in the philosophy courses he took in 1916 and 1917,[2] and it is also true that he claimed that during the summer that he was completing *The Great Gatsby* he was busy reading Oswald Spengler's *The Decline of the West (Letters* 289–90).[3] Altogether five references to Kant occur in his work prior to *The Great Gatsby,* one as early as 1915 in his short story "The Ordeal" (where Kant is mentioned along with Thomas Henry Huxley, Nietzsche, and Zola as crying *non serviam*), another one in "Benediction," developed out of the earlier story and published in 1920 (where the thick volumes of Kant are read along with those of Thomas Aquinas, Henry James Sr., and Cardinal Mercier by the seminarians), and one in chapter 3 of *This Side of Paradise* (where, in Amory's miniature satire "In a Lecture Room," Kant and General Booth may be said to define the range of the "broad and beaming view of truth" held by the pedant professors). Two more occur in *The Beautiful and Damned.* One is an incidental mention of the *Critique of Pure Reason* as a work whose study demands particular concentration. The other (a part of Maury Noble's nihilistic account of his futile quest for knowledge) is in fact a brief oblique allusion to the philosopher "infinitely removed from life staring at the tip of a steeple through the trees, trying to separate, definitely and for all time, the knowable from the unknowable" (*BD* 215).

While Fitzgerald's familiarity with the story of Kant and his church steeple, thus, may indeed go back to his early interest in philosophy, it was an event that occurred during the writing of *The Great Gatsby* that suggested Fitzgerald's use of the episode in the manuscript of his novel: the world-wide celebration, on April 22, 1924, of the bicentennial of Kant's birthday. Notable Festschriften, several memorial medals, and the dedication of an impressive open memorial hall built against the north wall of Königsberg Cathedral were the most conspicuous tributes to Kant's greatness upon this occasion. Bicentennial eulogies in newspapers and magazines included those in the *New York Times* and its *Book Review, The New Republic, The Nation,* and *The Literary Review,* among other American newspapers and journals. There is conclusive evidence that the event did not escape Fitzgerald's notice. By the middle of April 1924 the author had begun to work on the final version of *The Great Gatsby,* approaching what he had written in 1923 "from a new angle," as he told his editor, Maxwell Perkins, in a letter written about the tenth of the month (*Life in Letters* 67). Shortly thereafter a hiatus occurred in the writing while he was busy preparing the seventeen pieces of baggage that were to accompany him to Europe. The family sailed on May 3, making their way via Paris to the French Riviera, where the bulk of the manuscript of the novel was produced during the rest of the year. A few days before his departure, in its issue for April 30, 1924, *The New Republic* printed, as the second installment of Edmund Wilson's "Imaginary Conversations," a twelve-column dialogue between "Mr. Van Wyck Brooks and Mr. Scott Fitzgerald." In the fictitious exchange written by his friend from Princeton days, the author of *This Side of Paradise* acted as spokesman for the Younger Generation of American writers, congratulating Brooks, ten years his elder and the foremost critic of American letters at the time, on the occasion of the Dial Award. Wilson had him take the opportunity to plead for more attention to the work of contemporary authors, while Brooks appeared to be preoccupied with publishing chapters of his book on Henry James, second in the sequence of three cautionary tales in which the critic set out to explore and to illustrate the relationship between the American writer and his environment by reference to representative figures of the past. Fitzgerald and Wilson had seen each other frequently in the previous months (they had even discussed the plans for *The Great Gatsby*), and there is no doubt that Fitzgerald knew about the article and read it when it was published.[4] Getting to the end, he would have seen the headline of the contribution that followed, "Kant After Two Hundred Years," written by John Dewey, the noted American philosopher and educator. Regardless of whether Fitzgerald read Dewey's appraisal of Kant or not, its title directed his attention to the German philosopher and the bicentennial celebrations. More importantly, through the offices of his

friend Edmund Wilson, whom in 1936 he was to call his "intellectual con-
science," the author suddenly saw himself elevated, in the pages of a liberal
journal, to a conspicuous position in a notable constellation of intellectuals:
Van Wyck Brooks, John Dewey—and Immanuel Kant. Fitzgerald rose to the
occasion and decided to honor the metaphysician in his own way—by giving him a place in the manuscript of his novel. Regardless of its actual origin
and particular function in the text, the reference to Kant in the portion of
the manuscript that was written after the author's arrival in Europe (in a passage in chapter 5 of *The Great Gatsby* as published in 1925) must be taken to
be Fitzgerald's own deliberate bicentennial tribute to the great philosopher.

The bicentennial celebrations and the author's decision to include a reference to Kant in the manuscript came at a time when Fitzgerald had long
since determined that his novel was to be "something *new*—something extraordinary and beautiful and simple + intricately patterned" (*Correspondence*
112). It came at a time when he had also resolved "never [to] write another
document-novel" and announced his decision "to be a pure artist + experiment in form and emotion" (*Correspondence* 126). It also came at a time when
Fitzgerald may have begun to think that he rightfully belonged in the very
company that he found himself in in the pages of *The New Republic,* just a few
months before he announced to Perkins that he thought that his novel was
"about the best American novel ever written" (*Life in Letters* 80). *The Great
Gatsby,* therefore, unlike *This Side of Paradise* and *The Beautiful and Damned,* was
to be a novel of carefully selected and controlled detail and incident. Even if,
as scholars agree, it was to achieve "greatness through extensive proof revisions" (Bruccoli, "Introduction" xix), all details used in the manuscript version were clearly chosen with a view to the overall theme and structure of
the work. And even if, as the coincidental occurrence of the bicentennial
suggests, the reference to Kant may have grown out of the author's wish to
pay homage to the philosopher, it must be considered to be meant to serve
a definite purpose in whatever context it occurs in the novel. Just as Kant's
resting his eyes on the steeple of the Löbenicht church is not just the curious
habit of an eccentric dreamer, Fitzgerald's reference to the incident is not
just a convenient, perhaps deliberately erudite, comparison that the author
managed to insert in an opportune place.

For Kant, the habit of looking at the steeple invariably implied metaphysical reflection, and for Fitzgerald to choose to have his narrator use the comparison indicates that Nick Carraway is similarly engaged in philosophical contemplation. Making due allowance for the different types of discourse—that of the philosopher, almost entirely dispensing with example and metaphor; that of the novelist, almost entirely reasoning and persuading through example and metaphor—the passage in chapter 5 of *The Great Gatsby* that follows the reference to Kant is a deliberate discourse on Time and the inability of Man to escape its inexorable rule. Seemingly different from the precedent provided by Kant, for whom the Löbenicht church acted as the catalyst rather than as the object of contemplation, "Gatsby's enormous house" itself is what triggers Nick's train of thought. But, like Kant, the narrator in his reflections completely disregards the building as a physical presence while his discourse turns to the futility of the previous owner's high ambitions and the folly of his attempt to assert himself against Time: "A brewer had built it early in the 'period' craze, a decade before, and there was a story that he'd agreed to pay five years' taxes on all the neighboring cottages if the owners would have their roofs thatched with straw. Perhaps their refusal took the heart out of his plan to Found a Family—he went into an immediate decline. His children sold his house with the black wreath still on the door. Americans, while occasionally willing to be serfs, have always been obstinate about being peasantry" (*GG* 69).

The brewer appears to be an enterprising man with vision and energy. He builds a large mansion and sets out to "Found a Family," alliteration and the use of capital letters suggesting the traditional notion of a dynasty. His aristocratic and baronial cast of mind, along with his wealth, induce him to try to impose his will on his neighbors. His real antagonist is made out to be Time. Coming, as he does, from the "small muddy swamps and prehistoric marshes" produced by the rain on his irregular lawn, Nick seems to be struck by the utter briefness of the episode, all of which happened just a decade earlier. The brewer, he notes, went into "immediate decline," and the house was sold right upon his death. The attempt to conquer Time, to stop or even to turn back the clock, and the absolute futility of that attempt, even if supported by enormous riches, is suggested in such details as building a "period" house and endeavoring to reintroduce feudalism by restoring the environs to pastoral serenity and degrading the neighbors to peasants. The brewer's story, thus, turns out to be a perfect exemplum, the closest a narrative can come to being a philosophical text without actually leaving the realm of fiction. And the moral or the argument that it sustains is a resounding "You can't repeat the past!" Placed in the middle of chapter 5, at the point where Gatsby has just managed to meet Daisy after nearly five years of separation and now fully expects to be able to obliterate that period, the brief tale of the brewer momentarily halts the progress of the action to elucidate by its example Gatsby's quest as well as his failure. Placed in the middle of the narrative as a whole, moreover, Nick's view from Kant's window (various circumstances would seem to combine to endorse the appropriateness of the metaphor) echoes previous time references in the novel—notably the tilting of the defunct mantelpiece clock, in the same chapter—while simultaneously pointing forward to those that follow—notably the protagonist's refusal to accept the pastness of the past, in the next chapter. The facet of the brewer's children selling the house "with the black wreath still on the door," finally, foreshadows the end of both the protagonist and the novel. As is the case with other elements in *The Great Gatsby,* thematic and structural aspects thus work together to establish the significance of the detail of Fitzgerald's allusion to the German metaphysician. If—as critics have long maintained[5]— Joseph Conrad's *Almayer's Folly* may be assumed to have helped to shape the notion of Gatsby's house as a symbol of Gatsby's folly, then the author's adaptation of the anecdote of Kant and his steeple may be said to have helped the author to contain that notion in an emblematic scene designed to illuminate both the grandeur and the futility of Gatsby's quest. What may have been intended as a mere memorial tribute on the occasion of Kant's bicentennial has thus become an essential part of the intricate pattern of the novel.[6]

What Fitzgerald borrowed from the history of Western philosophy through the coincidence described above, his novel may be said to have repaid in full measure through a similar coincidence more than three quarters of a century later, for it was *The Great Gatsby* with its reference to Kant and his church steeple that induced me to look for the details of the view from Kant's window and which led to the recovery of the famous site in an unexpected shape. In the summer of 2001, I began—now that after nearly half a century Kaliningrad (as Königsberg is called today) had ceased to be closed to visitors— to trace its various components. But city maps, old and new, as well as sur-

viving landmarks and friendly residents were of no help in my search: all
of the elements that once made up the view from Kant's window had been
destroyed—in the bombings of August 1944, the land battle of 1945, the
aftermath of the war, and the reconstruction process. The house that as early
as 1893 had been built to replace the one Kant owned has disappeared, as has
Prinzessinstrasse, the very street on which it stood. The Löbenicht church
with its steeple succumbed to the 1944 air raids. The ruins of the old city
castle were dynamited in 1968 upon the express orders of Leonid Brezhnev,
only to be replaced by the ruins of the gigantic, uncompleted House of the
Soviets. Miraculously, the grave of Kant and the cenotaph in its open memorial hall that had been built against the north wall of the cathedral for the
1924 bicentennial survived the almost total destruction of the building itself. It is said that it was none other than Kant, who—because of the site of
his grave as well as his alleged role as a precursor of Marxist thinking—later
saved the ruins of the cathedral from suffering a similar fate to that of the city
castle. Today, the imposing edifice is being restored to serve as a multicultural
center. Along with a Russian Orthodox chapel, a small Protestant church, a
history museum, and an exhibit documenting the reconstruction process, the
building now houses a modest Immanuel Kant Museum, which was opened
in 1998.

It was here, after I had given up all hope of ever learning what Kant's view
from his window was like, that I met with a stroke of luck that is the reward
of any researcher's perseverance. The museum, in its third year of operation,
features the customary array of photos and documents, chiefly copies, as well
as editions of the writings of Kant in several languages, a wooden model of
his original house, and an imposing painting of one of his famous dinner
parties—all in all, sufficient items to occupy one for the 45 minutes a tour
guide will allow a busload of visitors to investigate the cathedral building as a
whole. When that time was up, and as I was walking toward the exit, I discovered in a large frame on the western wall three 9- x 12-inch pencil or char-
coal drawings of old Königsberg city sights, the remaining space being taken
up by detailed explanatory notes in Russian and German. One of the drawings bore the caption "Aussicht von Kant's Fenster"—"A View from Kant's
Window"—as well as the date 1936 and the signature "FL." Here, under glass,
was the view, the possible remnants of which I had been looking for in vain.

AUSSÍCHT VON KANT'S FENSTER

18. Friedrich Lahrs, "Aussicht von Kant's Fenster [A View From Kant's Window]," 1936. Immanuel Kant Museum, Kaliningrad "Cathedral" Museum, Courtesy of Wolfgang Blumers.

My good fortune did not end with this discovery: With the help of my tour guide, Mrs. Nadja Fetkewitsch, I was able to locate Mrs. Iraida Ostrogrudskaja, head of the museum. Through the medium of English as a *lingua franca,* as well as the courtesy of two guides serving as interpreters, I was able to explain my interest in the drawing and my purpose of making it available to the community of Fitzgerald scholars. We negotiated an agreement, part of which was that I provide editions of *The Great Gatsby* in English as well as in German, and late that night a messenger arrived at my hotel outside of the city with a copy of the drawing and express permission for its reproduction. The museum had gone to the trouble of taking the drawing out if its frame for a one-to-one Xerox reproduction and had also had a transcript made of the relevant section of the explanatory notes. My good fortune did not end here either: When I asked Mrs. Ostrogrudskaja who "FL" was, she told me that no one had yet been able to establish his identity. Much later, upon my return to Germany, I was able to ascertain that the explanatory notes were probably contemporaneous with the drawings and that in the section that

I had been given a reference was to be found to "my drawing," the possessive pronoun, without any doubt, referring to "FL." Since I did not want to publish the drawing without having at least tried to establish who "FL" was, I consulted with my colleague Walter T. Rix of the University of Kiel, who had negotiated an exchange with Königsberg University and had held teaching assignments there. He put me in touch with another expert on Königsberg, Professor Günter Brilla of Bonn, and it was his wife, Dr. Renate Brilla, who finally, through comparison with printed sources, produced evidence as incontrovertible as it was surprising. "FL" is the renowned architect Friedrich Lahrs (1880–1964), Professor at the Königsberg Academy from 1911 to 1934—the creator himself of the much-acclaimed Kant memorial hall of 1924, and a man whose achievement was held in honor even under Soviet rule by an the placement of a historic marker in Russian next to the monument. Also remembered as the author of a definitive study, *Das Königsberger Schloß* (1956), he had as early as 1926 been in charge of excavations to survey the castle site. Identifying "FL" as Friedrich Lahrs thus definitely enhances the value of the 1936 drawing of the view from Kant's window. But the good fortune resulting from such identification extends further, because it plainly saves the drawing from being minimized as rendering a mere "artist's impression." Rather, the drawing must be taken to betray a professional's eye for architectural detail and an accomplished expert's hand in its execution: this is what, at a distance of a little under half a mile, the steeple of the Löbenicht parish church looked like to Kant as his view passed by the north wall of the city castle with its round tower in the foreground and the heptagonal Haberturm in the middle distance. Through F. Scott Fitzgerald's *The Great Gatsby* of 1925, the account of Kant and his steeple had been brought home to where, in Ehregott Andreas Christoph Wasianski's *Kant in seinen letzten Lebensjahren* of 1804, it originated—only to find in Friedrich Lahrs's "Aussicht von Kant's Fenster" of 1936 the sole document to preserve for all time that important site in the history of Western philosophy, a uniquely significant configuration of details, every one of which has ceased to exist in reality.

Once by the Atlantic

Nick Carraway's Meditation on the Course of History and Its Ideological Context

When in the summer of 1923 Fitzgerald began to revamp a first draft of the beginning of the manuscript of his third novel, his deliberate attempt to write "something *new*—something extraordinary and beautiful and simple + intricately patterned" (*Correspondence* 112) eventually culminated in the act of moving his narrator's vision of "the old island [. . .] that flowered once for Dutch sailors' eyes" (*GG* 140) from an inconspicuous place at the end of chapter 1 to its capstone position at the very end of the book. The climactic conclusion of the narrative has drawn much attention, from countless readers, many critics, as well as not a few fellow writers. The suicide of Lilly Berry in John Irving's *The Hotel New Hampshire* (1981), committed out of despair for not being able to write something commensurate to Fitzgerald's ending, dramatizes and epitomizes the powerful appeal of the passage and its potential to engage the reader.

What is the secret of the enduring appeal of this ending? What is it that entices readers all over the world to respond to it with immediate acclaim? Most answers credit the evocative power of Fitzgerald's style. Evocative of what, however? There can be no doubt that the singular appeal of the ending lies in its deliberate evocation of both an archetypal situation and an archetypal experience: Man's epiphanic recognition of his own historicity, of his being placed in the stream of historical developments, as well as the narrator's resulting application of this lesson in a deliberate meditation on the destiny of his own nation. In the ending of *The Great Gatsby,* Fitzgerald finally and wholly transcends the role of the perceptive chronicler of contemporary events, even that of the enlightened historian, to assume the position of the sagacious philosopher of history.

This fact emerges more clearly once we examine the ending of the novel in the context of a number of similar dramatizations of the same archetypal experience, each of which can claim a prominent place in the history of Western thought and literature. There is sufficient evidence, moreover, that nearly all of these can actually be counted among Fitzgerald's potential sources of inspiration as he brought his text to a closure and in doing so made his bid to be admitted into the very circle of these renowned authors who had previously pondered the course of human history.

A convenient way to describe what happens when, on the last night before his return to the Midwest, Nick Carraway "wandered down to the beach" of Long Island Sound "and sprawled out on the sand" is to look at the scene in terms of cinematographic technique. The technique of dissolve had just been developed when Fitzgerald wrote his text, and as an early and ardent admirer of the movies he was certainly familiar with the process in which one image is slowly made to fade away while another one is forming to take its place. In transferring his scene from its original position in the manuscript, as well as in further revising it in proof, the author worked to bring out and to emphasize the slowness of the change that is taking place before his narrator's eyes. Three stages can thus be made out. The initial version reads: "as the moon rose higher the inessential houses seemed to melt away until I was aware of the old island here that flowered once for Dutch sailors' eyes" (*MS* 38). This is revised as follows: "as the moon rose higher the inessential houses themselves *began* to melt away until *suddenly I became* aware of the old island" (*MS* 257–58, emphasis added). And finally the adverb "suddenly" is replaced by "gradually" (*GG* 140). Slow to emerge, the resulting juxtaposition of the present and the past in two views of the same location of necessity implies discovery and acute awareness of the course of history: "the big shore places," "the inessential houses" of the present time, have taken the place of the trees that once had formed the "fresh, green breast of the new world" as perceived by "Dutch sailors' eyes." It is the identity of the view that propels the experience of historicity: the "vanished trees" are, as the author had stressed in the first draft of the passage, "the *very* trees that had made way for Gatsby's house" (*MS* 37, emphasis added). As much as inducing immediate awareness of the course of history, the juxtaposition of the two images impels spontaneous appraisal as expressed in the words and the imagery of Nick's account. The "big shore places" in all their solidity appear as merely "inessential houses," while the vanished trees had made up the "fresh, green breast of the new world." Such instantaneous appraisal gradually shades over into deliberate philosophical reflection about "the last and greatest of all human dreams" and the last encounter of man with "something commensurate to his capacity for wonder" (*GG* 140). Both these metaphors point to the idea of *translatio imperii*, the theory of the Westward Course of Empire that had given the American republic its special destiny and fostered the concept of American exceptionalism. Continuing to reason by metaphor, the narrator elects Gatsby to exemplify the nation's quest and its failure, as well as to demonstrate the nation's inability to face up to the reality of that failure: "He had come a long way to this blue lawn and his dream must have seemed so close that he could hardly fail to grasp it. He did not know that it was already behind him [. . .]" (*GG* 141). From focusing on Gatsby the text turns to the first person plural to voice communal delusion about America's golden future: "Gatsby believed in the green light, the orgastic future that year by year recedes before us. It eluded us then, but that's no matter—tomorrow we will run faster, stretch out our arms farther. . . . And one fine morning——." The empathetically spoken sentences in their incompleteness are indeed those of the deluded nation, its optimism not shared by the narrator in his role as the perspicacious philosopher. Nick Carraway retains his pessimism about the future of his nation to the very end, and yet he seems to count himself among the people described in the final metaphor of the novel: "So we beat on, boats against the current, borne back ceaselessly into the past."

The narrator in the final scene of *The Great Gatsby* thus appears as a sensitive individual to whom privileged information has come under auspicious circumstances. We find him at a turning point in his life, sprawled out on

19. *The Great Gatsby*, last page of the manuscript. Reproduced from *"The Great Gatsby": A Facsimile of the Manuscript*, p. 259.

the sand of the beach of Long Island Sound, open to the influences of nature and the cosmos, and his insight there, although entirely his own, yet comes to him as a kind of revelation. While it comes to him at what is the end of his stay on Long Island, it still turns out to be what is the actual beginning of his life as the historian of that period. Returning to the Midwest, he eventually starts to compose the "history of the summer" (*GG* 8) as an account of the events that lead up to and support the insight he has gained in that final moment of revelation.

∾

Archetypal scenes—such as we recognize Nick's final vision to be—by definition have no immediate literary sources. Still, as soon as we consider, not merely the constituent elements as they have been listed, but also their actual realizations and their thematic implications, an earlier rendition of the scene, its *locus classicus* as it were, readily suggests itself for comparison: Edward Gibbon's discovery of the central idea for his monumental *History of the Decline and Fall of the Roman Empire,* his famous "Capitoline vision," as it has come to be called. In his *Autobiography,* Gibbon gives the following account of it: "It was at Rome, on the 15th of October 1764, as I sat musing amidst the ruins of the Capitol, while the barefooted friars were singing vespers in the temple of Jupiter, that the idea of writing the decline and fall of the city first started to my mind" (124). Though stated in the briefest of terms, the incident yet contains all the major constituents as used by Fitzgerald. Past and present are juxtaposed in the ruins of the Capitol and a Roman temple on the one hand, and the friars' use of the temple for their Christian religious services on the other. The singing of the monks makes for the peculiar atmosphere that affects the historian as he sits musing upon what he observes. While the experience of historicity certainly was not new to him, the specific subject of the decline and fall of Rome (and eventually of the Roman empire itself) was the direct and immediate result of seeing material evidence of two historical epochs in direct juxtaposition. As with Nick Carraway, the finding of subject and theme was not the outcome of deliberate searching so much as it was an inspiration that came to a receptive mind at a fortuitous moment. While for Nick the date had been a special one even before his inspired vision, it is the inspiration itself that makes the date a special one for Gibbon, a day to remember ever afterward: October 15, 1764. But that date still had its significance to begin with, for he had long been looking forward to seeing Rome: "[. . .] at the distance of twenty-five years," as he wrote in his *Autobiography*, "I can neither forget nor express the strong emotions which agitated my mind as I first approached and entered the *eternal city*" (122).

Like Fitzgerald's narrator, Gibbon was anything but an impartial historian. His multivolume work turned out to call into question the ordinary view of history as a teleological progression. Rather, the general tendency of what he put to paper is summed up in his famous sentence, "I have described the triumph of barbarism and religion" (qtd. in Bury, "Introduction" vii). As "one of the great historical works of the Western world" (Bond 1), the *History of the Decline and Fall of the Roman Empire,* along with the author's *Autobiography,* the latter more popular still than the former, continued to be much read and quoted even in Fitzgerald's day. No evidence establishes definitively that Fitzgerald knew Gibbon, and yet it is interesting to speculate that the ending of *The Great Gatsby* may well have been written in full awareness of Gibbon's example, the very title of his work and its general tendency reinforcing Fitzgerald's analysis of the course of his own nation. But while Gibbon, at the end of the thirty-eighth chapter of his work, was still able to take "comfort in the thought that the flourishing colonies in America offer European civilization a secure refuge against any future barbarian invasions" (qtd. in Bond 20), Fitzgerald himself was far less certain about the course of history of what had long since become a republic of its own.

There is a curious piece of circumstantial evidence for Fitzgerald's interest in the English historian and his work, which also serves to demonstrate the author's general interest in history as a subject. During or following a visit to Fitzgerald in his Baltimore home in 1934, Bennett Cerf, one of the editors of the Modern Library, apparently commented on the small number of Modern Library editions among the author's books and offered to send him ten volumes as a present. Fitzgerald replied as follows on August 30: "Hey! do you think that I am so illiterate as to have only the few Modern Library books that are in the British-American section of fiction of my library? It is scattered all over the house at the moment, but in the different shelves of

history, philosophy, etc. I counted twenty-five after you left. For your stu-
pidity I am going to take you up on your offer, pick ten titles and ask you for
them. They are appended to this letter" (*Correspondence* 382).

The appended list included Suetonius, *Lives of the Twelve Caesars,* Modern
Library 188, as well as Gibbon, *History of the Decline and Fall of the Roman Empire,* Modern Library Giants 6 and 7 (neglecting to include #8, the third volume, probably through an oversight). While he may not have read Gibbon's
history at an earlier date, he must have known very well what he was asking for in his request. His subsequent use of the work in the construction of
the medieval world of his unfinished historical novel *Philippe, Count of Dark-
ness* points to the prominent place it was to occupy in Fitzgerald's "shelves
of history, philosophy, etc." (see Moreland 220 n12).

∾

Interestingly, Fitzgerald's request did not include *The Education of Henry
Adams,* a conspicuous item in the Modern Library ever since its publication
there in 1931, with an introduction by James Truslow Adams. This is additional, if purely circumstantial, evidence that he had owned a copy of the work
for much longer. At age 16, Fitzgerald had been introduced to the book's author in Washington, DC, by Father Fay and Shane Leslie. In *This Side of Paradise,* he had portrayed Adams as Thornton Hancock and shown his protagonist, Amory Blaine, for a time to come under the influence of his work, much
like Blaine's creator had. In his 1921 review of John Dos Passos's *Three Soldiers,* Fitzgerald had shown his familiarity with the work of the older author
by calling John Andrews, the principal protagonist, "a little too much the ultimate ineffectual, the Henry Adams-in-his-youth sort of character" (*FSF on
Authorship* 49). Many scholars, moreover, have found *The Beautiful and Damned*
of 1922 to have been similarly colored by his encounter with the historian.[1]
If, then, Fitzgerald had not discovered Gibbon on his own by the time he
wrote the ending of *The Great Gatsby,* he had probably done so through *The
Education of Henry Adams.* In a passage in chapter 6, devoted to Adams's stay
in Rome in May 1860, the author describes himself as following in the footsteps of Gibbon and quotes a slightly embellished version of the above paragraph from the latter's *Autobiography.* This version is even closer to the scene

as rendered in *The Great Gatsby,* in that it has Gibbon, like Nick Carraway, have his experience late in the evening, as well as in a church building that actually and materially epitomizes the age that followed the Roman Empire. As quoted from John Murray's *Handbook for Rome and Its Environs,* this variant passage in the *Education* runs as follows: "in the close of the evening, as I sat musing in the Church of the Zoccolanti or Franciscan Friars, while they were singing Vespers in the Temple of Jupiter, on the ruins of the Capitol" (91). Walking around Rome and sitting where Gibbon had sat a century earlier, seeing what Gibbon had seen then, and asking Gibbon's "Why?" Henry Adams lived through and, by putting it on paper, gave to the world another classic version of the archetypal experience of historicity. He, too, although still a young man and a mere tourist, with "the thought of posing for a Gibbon" never yet entering his mind (92), was to become a historian. And again it was the experience of the Eternal City, the Rome of antiquity as well as the Rome of the Middle Ages, that was instrumental in bringing about that decision. The juxtaposition, in his own work, of virgin and dynamo as symbols of 13th-century unity and twentieth-century multiplicity, in chapter 25 of the *Education*—as well as in his complementary studies of *Mont-Saint-Michel and Chartres* (1904; 1913) and in the *Education* as a whole, along with the posthumous publication in 1919 of speculative historical essays as *The Degradation of the Democratic Dogma,* a title chosen by his brother Brooks Adams—did much to suggest that Henry Adams had entertained the same kind of pessimistic view of the course of American history as that which was to inform the musings of Nick Carraway in the final scene of *The Great Gatsby.* Adams's ironic stylizing of his education as a series of failures, moreover, along with his suggestion that Gibbon's question about the reasons for the collapse of Rome might well have to be asked about America, too, supported such reading of his work in the years after World War I: "Why! Why!! Why!!! [. . . .] No one ever had answered the question to the satisfaction of any one else; yet every one who had either head or heart, felt that sooner or later he must make up his mind what answer to accept. *Substitute the word America for the word Rome,*" Henry Adams concluded, "*and the question became personal*" (92, emphasis added).

≈

On June 6, 1940, in the first year of World War II, Fitzgerald wrote to Maxwell Perkins to thank him for a book by J. F. C. Fuller, *Decisive Battles: Their Influence upon History and Civilisation,* which had just been published by Scribner's. In discussing the 1,060-page work, Fitzgerald refers to the "curious philosophic note which began to run through it" and goes on expertly to discuss Oswald Spengler's *The Decline of the West,* which had been touched on by Fuller. And Fitzgerald continues as follows: "Did you ever read Spengler— specifically including the second volume? I read him the same summer I was writing *The Great Gatsby* and I don't think I ever quite recovered from him. He and Marx are the only modern philosophers that still manage to make sense in this horrible mess—I mean make sense by themselves and not in the hands of distorters" (*Letters* 289–90). Fitzgerald's claim to have read Spengler while writing *The Great Gatsby* has been disputed, since *The Decline of the West* was not available in English translation until 1926. There actually is an interview statement by Fitzgerald that points to 1926 as the year in which he first read the work (see note 37). But Richard D. Lehan has pointed out that there were several commentaries on *The Decline of the West* prior to the publication of the novel and identified "an 8,000-word essay by W. K. Stewart in *Century* magazine" as Fitzgerald's probable early source of information on Spengler (*The City in Literature* 212 n3).[2] Stewart's 10-page article, "The Decline of Western Culture: Oswald Spengler's 'Downfall of Western Civilization' Explained," appeared in the September 1924 issue of *Century* magazine. It was available by August 20 and could just have reached Fitzgerald in Europe and been read by him before he completed his manuscript in October of the same year. Stewart provides a succinct summary and explication of both volumes of *Der Untergang des Abendlandes,* stressing the philosophical aspect of the work that Fitzgerald found to be its fascinating feature. Lehan has shown (in working from the later English translation of the complete text rather than from Stewart's summary) that "much in Spengler appealed directly to Fitzgerald's personal sense of mental and physical instability, of dissipation and weariness" (211), and that a whole range of "Spenglerian ideas infuse *The Great Gatsby*" (212). Confining ourselves to the summary that Fitzgerald actually could have read in 1924, as well as to the scene of Nick's final vision as the archetypal experience under scrutiny, we find one

passage in particular in Stewart's article that proves illuminating. Having explained that Spengler rejects the idea that the curve plotted for the course
of history was ever upward—and also that each indigenous culture that de-
velops in the course of history passes through childhood, youth, manhood,
and old age—there is the following description of what by implication he
finds to be the present situation of the Western world: "The ultimate fate of
each culture [. . .] is to lapse into a petrified civilization, in which condition
it may last on indefinitely, like the Chinese or the Egyptian, outwardly enduring, but inwardly dead. The contrast between a culture and a civilization
has long been familiar to the Germans, but Spengler is apparently the first
to make the distinction a chronological one. A culture is naïve and spontaneous, full of creative energy, and largely a thing of the heart and the will.
In a civilization the creative impulse is exhausted, and the intellect becomes
dominant; life grows mechanized, it centers in great cities, so that men lose
touch with the soil and with their ancestral myths; skepticism supervenes,
and the higher life becomes sterile, though bodily comforts are more fully
gratified than ever" (590).

While some of the points made here refer back to earlier sections in *The
Great Gatsby,* it is the contrast between city and country as typifying civilization versus culture that underlies and shapes the dramatization of Nick's vision. The inessential houses and the city ("the tall incandescent city on the
water," as Fitzgerald first wrote to give the metropolis an appropriate Baby-
lonian connotation [*MS* 38]) are foregrounded against the dark fields of the
republic "on the other side of the city" (*MS* 259), as Fitzgerald put it before
he chose the word "beyond" as the more resonant preposition. Through the
course of Gatsby's life as recapitulated here by Nick Carraway, the spatial
opposition between city and country is transformed into a temporal opposition, just as Spengler, in Stewart's reading, had been the first to make the distinction between city-centered civilization and rural-based culture a chronological one. Gatsby's dream was conceived and it was lost in the past, it had
a rural origin, it belonged with the early years of the republic: "He did not
know that it was already behind him, somewhere back in that vast obscurity
beyond the city, where the dark fields of the republic rolled on under the
night" (*GG* 141). This ending with its overtones of Spenglerian doom is in

full accordance with Fitzgerald's celebration of a pastoral America of simpler values throughout what has been called his fable of East and West. In having Nick return to the Midwest the author passes judgment on civilization in the East along the lines of Spengler's system of values, fully aware, though, that the course of history cannot be reversed.

Two years after the publication of *The Great Gatsby,* when *The Decline of the West* had definitely become his "bed-book" (Salpeter 275), the author allowed himself to be discussed under the caption "Fitzgerald, Spenglerian." In an interview published in the April 3, 1927, issue of the *New York World,* Harry Salpeter provided many quotations that indicate the author's pessimism about the future of his nation and civilization in general. In their totality these remarks constitute the discursive equivalent of the message contained in the ending of *The Great Gatsby.* It is interesting to note that in the kind of mysticism to which Spengler's ideas seem to have given rise in many quarters, Fitzgerald saw hope for his nation "in the birth of a hero who will be of age when America's testing comes" and that most likely "he will come out of the immigrant class, in the guise of an east-side newsboy" (Salpeter 277)—much like the protagonist of *The Great Gatsby,* whose immigrant background (as the revised account of the genesis of the novel as given would seem to emphasize) is essential to an adequate reading of the text.

∾

The dark fields of the republic—and the promises they held for a golden future for America—had as early as 1833 been the subject of a historical meditation similar to the ones that have been considered, with the difference that in this case the juxtaposition is one of present and future as much as of present and past. In "The Prairies," a well-known poem inspired by his visit to Illinois during the previous year, William Cullen Bryant has the narrator take a solitary ride on horseback across an endless expanse of land, the very description of which seems to explain as well as implement Fitzgerald's image of "the dark fields of the republic" that "rolled on under the night." In a panegyric style not unlike that of the measured and cadenced prose of the ending of *The Great Gatsby,* Bryant, like Fitzgerald, celebrates a uniquely

American subject, deliberately stressing its Americanness in the very open-ing: "These are the gardens of the Desert, these / The unshorn fields, bound-less and beautiful, / For which the speech of England has no name— / The Prairies" (all quotations from the poem as printed in *The New Oxford Book of American Verse*). In describing "the encircling vastness" as taken in by the recep-tive spectator with swelling heart and dilated sight, every effort is made to have the scene appear, not stationary, but animated and responsive. The prai-ries stretch "in airy undulations," like an ocean, the "rounded billows fixed." Then, by "breezes of the South," they are unchained again: "the surface rolls and fluctuates to the eye." But the image, although fitting and sustained, and indeed bearing some relation to that chosen by Fitzgerald, is hardly as ar-resting as that of "the dark fields of the republic" that "rolled on under the night," particularly since with Fitzgerald the metaphor cannot be construed to be a visual one at all.

The "hollow beating" of the footsteps of his steed make the narrator "think of those / Upon whose rest he tramples." What follows is an imaginary ac-count of the fate of two Indian civilizations, that of the mound builders and that of the roaming hunter tribes. The latter vanquished the former before they, in turn, were uprooted by the white man. A third section of the poem is given over to presenting the philosophy of history derived from this sur-vey: "Thus change the forms of being. Thus arise / Races of living things, glorious in strength, / And perish, as the quickening breath of God / Fills them, or is withdrawn." The conclusion is not unlike that offered by Gib-bon, Adams, or Spengler, except that in Bryant's lines it is God who is iden-tified as the agent at work in the process of change. And another difference emerges in the fourth section of the poem, which presents the imaginative view of a prospective new civilization on the prairie, that of the white man. The latter's "advancing multitude" is portended by the bee, "a more adven-turous colonist than man," with whom he crossed the Atlantic to "hide his sweets, as in the golden age, / Within the hollow oak." Bryant wrote at a time, and of a time, when the dark fields of the republic were still a virgin land, the fertile seedbed of the dream of an agrarian society, of precisely the kind of rural society whose demise Fitzgerald was to lament. It is not at all unlikely that Fitzgerald was familiar with "The Prairies." But in Fitzgerald's own philosophy of history, Bryant's poem could have served him as merely a negative foil, both for the image of the dark fields of the republic and for the view of America's future.

~

The text that comes closest to the ending of *The Great Gatsby* in its presentation of the archetypal experience of historicity and its theory of history is Matthew Arnold's "Dover Beach," written about the middle of the nineteenth century and first published in 1867. As Arnold's best-known poem, it is highly unlikely not to have been encountered by Fitzgerald as early as in his Princeton years. His appreciation of Arnold as a poet seems to have endured. The Rare Books Collection in the university library of his alma mater preserves a copy of *The Poetical Works of Matthew Arnold,* inscribed by Fitzgerald, in the last year of his life, for Sheilah Graham: "Sheila from Scott with Love 1940."

"Dover Beach" is a dramatic monologue, but unlike in the poems of Robert Browning, the master of that form, there is no discernible mask. The speaker is the poet himself, and the views expressed are those of Arnold. Although he finds himself inside a room rather than in the open, and although he invites his beloved to join him at the window, the details of what he sees and their arrangement are remarkably like those that Nick sees and observes: "The sea is calm to-night. / The tide is full, the moon lies fair / Upon the straits;—on the French coast the light / Gleams and is gone; the cliffs of England stand, / Glimmering and vast, out in the tranquil bay" (all quotations from the poem as printed in *The New Oxford Book of English Verse*). An auditory perception, the "grating roar of pebbles," alternately drawn back by the waves and then flung "up high the strand," brings "the eternal note of sadness in." As in Fitzgerald's text, the subsequent reflection on the course of history is tinged with nostalgia for the past. The narrator himself is aware of the archetypal situation in which he finds himself, and by association is led to think of Sophocles at the Ægæan pondering "the turbid ebb and flow / Of human misery." In his own meditation, he, too, takes the sea and the full tide for his text and, in juxtaposing past and present, continues as follows: "The Sea of Faith / Was once, too, at the full, and round earth's shore / Lay like the folds of a bright girdle furled. / But now I only hear / Its melancholy, long, withdrawing roar, / Retreating, to the breath / Of the night-wind, down the vast edges drear / And naked shingles of the world." The present, he concludes, "Hath really neither joy, nor love, nor light, / Nor certitude, nor peace, nor help for pain." His lament about the loss of a unifying idea and a compelling center, a familiar theme in all of Arnold's work, echoes or anticipates the findings of Gibbon, Adams, and Spengler, even though Gibbon had not brought his investigation up to the present time and had presented Christianity as a destructive rather than a positive force. The concluding lines of the poem are a powerful and telling metaphor for Arnold's deep pessimism regarding the state of contemporary culture and religious faith: "And we are here as on a darkling plain / Swept with confused alarms of struggle and flight, / Where ignorant armies clash by night." In its movement from the narrator's responsive perception of a serene view of nature to his ensuing profound reflection on the course of human history, the archetypal experience of historicity as presented by Matthew Arnold is much like that of Fitzgerald, also in that its sustained poetic quality culminates in a memorable metaphor. Both the image of the darkling plain and that of the boats against the current grows out of the details of the scene as taken in by the narrator and then proceeds to unite the two levels of sensory perception and philosophic reflection. In all the effortlessness of their development, they yet stand out as transcending achievements in these two renditions of archetypal experience and are intricately bound up with their exemplification of shattered certainties. In fact, the remarkable vogue of the "darkling plain" and the "boats against the current," along with the "dark fields of the republic," as titles for either novels, stories, plays, poems, and poetry collections, as well as song lyrics and even scholarly studies, is probably partly due to this very fact and the resulting appeal to modernists.

Placing Fitzgerald's meditation on the course of history in the context of similar meditations does not mean to challenge the originality of the ending of *The Great Gatsby*. Although the attempt has been made to suggest that he could have been familiar with—or at least aware of—the various texts that have been considered, Fitzgerald certainly developed the conclusion of his novel from its own specific premises. But in all of his work, as well as in his correspondence and conversation, he readily and eagerly responded to the work of other writers and to intellectual currents and social trends and fads.[3] His library, as has been indicated, included what he called "shelves of history, philosophy, etc." besides "the British-American section of fiction." He must have been familiar, therefore, with the terms *decline, fall, unity, multiplicity, failure, degradation,* and others, along with their specific implications and connotations. And he must have considered these in his own thinking about history and philosophy as well as in his writing. The story of Gatsby as Fitzgerald had developed it out of an earlier draft in the light of what he witnessed, experienced, and learned during his residence on Long Island and frequent visits to New York City, in close proximity to the very rich as well as to liberal intellectuals, must have made him see that the list of terms provided in the philosophies of his elders was fully applicable to *Civilization in the United States*, regardless of whatever actual use he himself may have made of their texts. No one should underestimate his power to appropriate, and at the same time in his fiction to supersede, suggestions received from others. In *The Great Gatsby* he did more than that, however. In having Nick Carraway, in his final vision on the beach of Long Island Sound, talk about the protagonist and his failure in terms of Gatsby's dream, he imaginatively and clairvoyantly anticipated James Truslow Adams, who is credited with having introduced, in *The Epic of America* of 1931, the term *The American Dream* into modern discourse and then examined the degradation of that dream in contemporary materialism. The least that the texts that have been considered in conjunction with the ending of *The Great Gatsby* do is to highlight Fitzgerald's intense awareness of, and his sensitivity to, the intellectual currents of his time and the great tradition of Western thought as well as his imaginative, creative, highly personal, and thoroughly unique responses to them.

Notes

Chapter 1

1. See Walbridge, *Literary Characters Drawn from Life*: "It has already been broadly hinted that Edmund Wilson Jr., when he introduced a disturbing young novelist in his play [. . .] was only getting even for a suspected caricature of himself in 'The Beautiful and Damned.'—Alexander Woolcott in the *New York Sun*" (110).

2. The actual Julius Fleischmann (1871–1925) and his brother Max (1877–1952), like all members of the family who owned the Fleischmann Yeast Company, retained the German spelling (-nn) of the name. Wilson's use of "Fleischman" could perhaps be seen as a halfhearted attempt to veil (as well as to reveal) the identity of the real-life model.

3. There is conflicting information about who was the builder of The Lindens in 1910. Klieger, in *The Fleischmann Yeast Family* (2004) (p. 49), as well as other sources, name Julius, while Raymond E. and Judith A. Spinzia in their exhaustive study *Long Island's Prominent North Shore Families: Their Estates and Their Country Homes* (2004) (vol. 1, p. 566) list Max as the owner who also contracted for the original construction. The question is of some relevance for Fitzgerald biography as well as the study of the genesis of *The Great Gatsby*. Since Max seems to have been the owner, the likelihood is greater that Fitzgerald actually visited Sands Point and saw The Lindens as well as perhaps August Belmont's Beacon Towers and Malcolm Douglas Sloane's Lands End. These were mansions of particular renown in a choice and ex-

clusive neighborhood that later in the decade attracted and admitted people such as Mary Harriman Rumsey, Tommy Hitchcock, and Herbert Bayard Swope—all three of whom, incidentally, were friends of the Fitzgeralds who played an important role in the gestation of *The Great Gatsby*.

4. The endpaper page from Malraux's *Man's Hope* is reproduced in *F. Scott Fitzgerald's "The Great Gatsby": A Documentary Volume*, p. 55, as well as in Bruccoli's "Introduction" to *The Great Gatsby*, p. xiv, and his "Introduction" to *The Great Gatsby: A Facsimile of the Manuscript*, p. xvii. References to parties on Long Island that Fitzgerald attended are to be found in his *Ledger*, pp. 177–78, as well as in Goldstein, pp. 26–27.

5. Undated TS note by Arthur Mizener [c. 1951–1954]. The 3- x 5-inch note, apparently written by Mizener to identify the correspondent for his letter files, begins as follows: "Max von Guerlach was, in the 1920s, the Long Island bootlegger who, in a general way, gave FSF his first conception of Gatsby's career."

6. Undated letter from Max von Gerlach to Arthur Mizener, sent after Gerlach had moved to the Mansfield Hotel at 12 West 44th Street, c. 1953–1954, as well as letter of June 10, 1954, from Belle Trenholm (for Gerlach) to Arthur Mizener (Arthur Mizener Papers, Princeton University Library).

7. Belle Trenholm wrote to Arthur Mizener, "Max [. . .] 'lives alone' and 'dies alone.' He has stopped drinking and *giving parties*. Says it's a 'different world.' His mind is alert. [. . .] He says he literally lives in pajamas—at home most of the time." She goes on to plead with Mizener to respond in some way: "[. . .] a new personality, at present, would be a '*mind*' send to him. [. . .] Do write Max 'ir' regardless of Great Gads or what nots" (see note 6).

8. The letter was written in response to Shane Leslie's "Some Memories of Scott Fitzgerald" (*Times Literary Supplement*, October 31, 1958, p. 632) and was published in that paper on November 14, 1958, p. 657. A copy of the November 5, 1958, letter is in the Arthur Mizener Papers, Princeton University Library (Box 2, Folder 20).

9. For a recent instance, see Jonathan P. Fegley's identification of "Gatsby's historical models, the Long Island bootlegger Max Gerlach and the New York stock swindler Edward M. Fuller" (131).

10. Lydia is not listed in the 1900 Federal Census Record; the record also indicates that her mother, Elizabeth, had given birth to five children, three of whom were living when the census was taken as of June 1, 1900 (1900 United States Federal Census).

11. Arriving in New York City early in 1911, Max still gave his address as 841 North 40th Avenue, Chicago, Illinois (Ship Manifest of *SS St. Paul*). In his 1914 Berlin

passport application he also stated that he and his mother had lived in Chicago as well as New York City (Gerlach Passport Application 1914).

12. Ordnance Department Personalia Sheet, August 6, 1918, plus additional information from city directories and other documents. The information has since been supplemented by Daniel Strohl, and Strohl also found "a Max Stark as an incorporator of the American Auto Supply Co. in New York in 1909" ("Bootleggers, Used Car Dealers and *The Great Gatsby*").

13. On his Berlin Embassy Passport Application of August 1914 he gave 369 Sterling Avenue, Joliet, Illinois, as his address.

14. He used the name of Gerlach as early as on the ship manifest of the *SS St. Paul*, sailing from Southampton the end of 1910. He returned to the name Stork on the ship manifest of the *SS Saratoga*, sailing from Havana, Cuba, about two months later. Stork eventually became the favored middle name, used alternately with "A" for his stepfather's given name as a middle initial. Gerlach's lack of consistency in the use of a family name would seem to reflect conflicting national and personal loyalties as they are discussed below, on his own part toward others as much as possibly on the part of others toward himself. The copy of his photo among a total of 1,326 images in the New York police department evidence collection for the years from 1915 to the 1930s, accessed from the police department's crime scene laboratory and made available online in April 2012 (New York City Municipal Archives Online Gallery: pde_0368), is wholly detached from whatever case file in which it belonged. But the date of the copy, July 8, 1915, is just two months after that of the sinking of the *Lusitania* by a German submarine. Gerlach's brush with the police (as Max Stork), therefore, may well reflect the burgeoning anti-German sentiment that, for him, was to culminate in the report of June 29, 1917, to the Bureau of Investigation, US Department of Justice, *in re* his alleged "German Activities," as well as the report prepared in 1918 by the American Protective League.

15. See note 27.

16. The information stems from an entry in the New York Passenger Lists, 1820–1957. Passport application files for the period from 1925 to the present are not open to the public. The US Department of State Passport Services, Law Enforcement Liaison Division, at Washington, DC, has not been able to fill my repeated requests for a copy of the passport application. Inspection of the document would have been of great help in closing the information gap that exists about Max Gerlach in the 1920s.

17. All information taken from reports of Gerlach's suicide attempt in the *Long Island Star-Journal* of December 22, 1939 ("Car Dealer Dying; Shot Self in Head: Von Gerlach Tries Suicide in Village Apartment"), and December 23, 1939 ("Would-Be

Suicide Is Still Critical: Von Gerlach's Condition Shows No Change"). The items were located by Howard G. Comen of the Comen Detective Agency, Charleston, South Carolina, who has kindly made them available to me. Gerlach's suicide was also reported in the *New York Herald Tribune* ("Pair Sit Reading Papers, Then He Shoots Himself," December 22, 1939) and in the *New York World Telegraph* ("Calls on Friend, Attempts Suicide," December 22, 1939).

18. All information taken from the burial records of Max Stork Gerlach, October 30, 1958, Frank E. Campbell, Inc., New York City. The assistance of Mr. Cesare Mannino is gratefully acknowledged.

19. Passport Application #01584 of August 4, 1914, to the American Embassy at Berlin by Max A. Gerlach. Unless otherwise noted, all subsequent information in this section stems from this one-page document.

20. The town of Norderney in Lower Saxony, as the most likely place referred to, has searched all civil and church records without finding a trace of Gerlach or his family. I gratefully acknowledge the assistance of Mrs. Bettina Mai, Mr. Manfred Bätje, and Mrs. Elisabeth Hillmann of the Town of Norderney, Niedersachsen (Standesamt, Stadtarchiv, Ev. Luth. Kirche).

21. H. W. Grunewald, June 29, 1917, Bureau of Investigation report, Department of Justice, *in re* Max Gerlach, German Activities. Old German Files, 1909–1921, Case No. 8000-33016, Case Title: German Activities. Unless otherwise noted, all subsequent information in this section stems from this two-page document.

22. Max Gerlach, Ordnance Department Personalia Sheet, August 6, 1918, Record Group 156, National Archives and Records Administration II, College Park, Maryland. Unless otherwise noted, all subsequent information in this section stems from this one-page document.

23. National Archives and Records Administration, Record Group 59: State Department Passport Applications, Max Gerlach, #140599, November 15, 1919, Vol. 2302, 2 pages. Unless otherwise noted, all subsequent information in this section stems from this two-page document.

24. Thomas Dilworth has noted the impact of the Arrow Collar advertising campaign on the characterization of Jay Gatsby and the world of Fitzgerald's novel. Going by the photo of his passport application, Gerlach did look "like Arrow Collar ads," a "1920s simile" used to depict a "well-heeled, well-groomed, nattily dressed, handsome young man" (83), and would have reinforced whatever impact the campaign had on the author's work.

25. See note 49. As James W. Gerard notes in *My Four Years in Germany*, "By custom in Germany, a 'von' when he goes abroad is allowed to call himself Baron" (http://net.lib.byu.edu/estu/wwi/memoir/Gerard/4yrs2.htm net).

26. The report of his suicide attempt in the *New York Herald Tribune* of December 22, 1939, states that "he held a major's commission in the Ordnance Department at the time of his action." The information seems to have been provided by Miss Elizabeth Mayer, in whose apartment at 10 Jones Street he shot himself.

27. The charges were for selling four drinks of whiskey (March 7, 1927), selling four drinks of whiskey, as well as possessing 19 bottles Scotch whiskey, 3 bottles gin, 1 bottle Bacardi rum, 1 bottle Holland gin, 2 bottles Chartreuse, 1 bottle Champagne, 1 bottle three-fourths full of alcohol, and possessing "a quantity of labels, corks and tops" (March 9, 1927). The fine in this instance was $200. Another charge was for possessing 1 quart bottle half filled with whiskey (July 24, 1927), the fine was $10. Both cases were heard in the US District Court for the Southern District of New York, Court Dockets #46-768 and #48-225. In current purchasing power the fines would amount to $2,680 and $134, respectively (www.measuringworth .com).

28. My attempts to identify Gerlach as an actual yacht owner or yacht broker have failed. He was not a member of the patrician New York Yacht Club, nor is his name to be found in any of the 1920 to 1932 volumes of *Lloyd's Register of Yachts* or in *Yachting* magazine. I gratefully acknowledge the assistance of Vanessa Cameron, librarian and archivist at the New York Yacht Club.

29. According to information received from Dan Hardy, Rice "bought, owned and operated the first automobile ever seen in the [Philippines]" (4). In 1916 he drove a "big Hudson" in New York City (6), and "[a]ccording to an account written in the fall of 1918" Rice during his years in Havana owned "a gigantic touring car and two racers" (6) ("Kandiyohi County Adventurer Cushman Rice—The Image of Gatsby," 12-page manuscript draft of September 14, 2004). See also Dan Hardy's "Cushman Rice: The Man Who Was Gatsby?" about Rice's lifestyle and his "expensive automobiles" (4).

30. Pietrusza's section on "The Players in Our Drama" has the following entry on Bauchle: "Wastrel heir to the Y&S licorice fortune. Arnold Rothstein's front man at the Partridge Club, Manhattan's poshest floating card game" (ix); see also Pietrusza 94–95.

31. Barbara Probst Solomon's "Westport Wildlife" appeared in *The New Yorker,* September 9, 1996, pp. 78–85. I gratefully acknowledge her assistance as well as that of Deborah A. Celia, reference librarian of the Westport Public Library, and Katie Chase and Richard Webb of the Westport Historical Society.

32. Related fictional uses of a Rolls-Royce automobile are to be found in Ginevra King's story written as a response to Fitzgerald's "The Perfect Hour" ("Her 'Rolls-Royce' was waiting [. . .]" [West 52]) and in Zelda Fitzgerald's *Save Me the Waltz* (the

metaphor of "a Rolls-Royce thread" [71]; the rich Nordika "came to her lessons in a Rolls-Royce" [154]).

33. Fitzgerald's monthly budget for 1923 included $80 for "House Liquor" (Bruccoli, *Some Sort of Epic Grandeur,* 2nd ed., 188n), amounting to a little over $1,000 in current purchasing power (www.measuringworth.com). In assessing what seems a large sum, some allowance must be made for Prohibition prices.

34. Mizener's account of Heywood Broun's telling John Peale Bishop about a scheme to have Fitzgerald "do a part-time column for *The World* at $125 a week if he wanted a chance to look for material" reflects the author's concern and its apparent currency among friends (*The Far Side of Paradise* 148–49).

35. The passage in *A Book of Prefaces* reads as follows: "'Conrad,' says Walpole, 'is of the firm and resolute conviction that life is too strong, too clever and too remorseless for the sons of men.'" To make the statement applicable to Dreiser as well, Mencken had suggested to delete the word "clever" and to substitute "stupid" or "unintelligible." It is in the deletion of "clever" that Fitzgerald follows Mencken and thus acknowledges the authority of Mencken's text (see H. L. Mencken, "Theodore Dreiser," in *A Book of Prefaces* [1916] as reprinted in *The Vintage Mencken* 48).

36. F. Scott Fitzgerald, "'Ten Best Books I Have Read': *The Philosophy of Friedrich Nietzsche* (H. L. Mencken) [1908]. A keen, hard intelligence interpreting the Great Modern Philosopher" (86). A newspaper article titled "Scott Fitzgerald Lays Success to Reading," published during Fitzgerald's first visit to Hollywood in early 1927 and preserved as a clipping in his scrapbook (now in the F. Scott Fitzgerald Papers, Princeton University Library), contains his list of "10 best books" ("one for each two years [. . .], the books I have read that have been the greatest influence on my mind"), which includes "At 24, 'The Genealogy of Morals'—Friedrich Nietzsche. [. . .] At 28, Ludendorff's 'Memoirs.' At 30, 'The Decline of the West'—Oswald Spengler" (Millen 83).

37. While there is sufficient evidence in his correspondence that Fitzgerald read Spengler's *The Decline of the West,* he could not have done so at the time of the writing of *The Great Gatsby.* Spengler's work did not appear in English translation until 1926. And there is in fact a 1927 interview in which Fitzgerald correctly and unambiguously stated that he first read Spengler's work when he was age 30, i.e., after the date of its first appearance in English translation (see the preceding note, "Scott Fitzgerald Lays Success to Reading" [Millen 83]). But there were magazine articles as early as 1924 that reviewed and analyzed Spengler's theory in detail and thus account for Fitzgerald's awareness of the philosopher when he was writing his novel. See chapter 4, "Once by the Atlantic. . . ."

38. He must have found it a curious coincidence, however, when he learned

that, quite like Gerlach, William Louis Sonntag Jr., the subject of Dreiser's "W. L. S." sketch, had been claiming a baronial title and that becoming an actual baron was among the "dreams [. . .] so near fulfillment" (359) at the time of his premature death from fever contracted while on assignment in the Spanish-American war.

39. In reviewing a draft of Edmund Wilson's "Literary Spotlight" analysis of Fitzgerald's career for publication in the March 1922 *Bookman,* the author insisted, "I'm not Irish on Father's side [. . .]". Bruccoli finds this claim "curious as well as incorrect": "Fitzgerald's attempt to rewrite his pedigree supports Wilson's theory that his erratic behavior resulted from his social insecurity as an Irish Catholic" (*Some Sort of Epic Grandeur,* second rev. ed. 160). For further details about Fitzgerald's interest in questions of race and ethnicity at the time of his work on the novel see chapter 2, "Dinner at the Buchanans': Beginning *The Great Gatsby*."

40. The same observation is made by Matthew J. Bruccoli, "Introduction," *GG* xix n20.

41. The sentence, in slightly different form, was transferred to page 69 of the manuscript but then not carried over into the galley version.

42. The insertion of "no" in the first sentence is called for by the context of this paragraph (which was obviously copied by the author from an earlier version) as well as the manuscript as a whole and by Perkins's response to it.

43. In doing so, Fitzgerald may well have been aware, though, of another case of somewhat curious precedence in Dreiser's *Twelve Men.* In his sketch "My Brother Paul," Dreiser had described a chance encounter on Broadway on Christmas Eve between himself and his brother, Paul Dresser: "'Now, see here, sport,' he began—a favorite expression of his, 'sport'" (86); and a few pages down Paul is heard to refer to his brother specifically as "old sport here" (89).

44. As has been mentioned previously, the Ordnance Department Personalia sheet indicates that Gerlach's application had been for captain, but both his commission and honorable discharge were as first lieutenant.

45. Here Fitzgerald is known to have drawn on the experiences of a Great Neck resident, on the exemplary war record of the "patrician war hero and polo star Tommy Hitchcock," whom he idolized throughout his life (see Meyers 103 and Bruccoli, *Some Sort of Epic Grandeur* 184n).

46. See Bruccoli, *GG* 188–89, explanatory notes for p. 39, lines 20–22, as well as James H. Meredith's searching account of the importance of Fitzgerald's endeavor to construct "a plausible combat record" (183) for his protagonist (180–86).

47. Fitzgerald's own interest (and possible membership) in the American Legion is reflected in *The Beautiful and Damned* in "a mimeographed notice urging 'the boys' in condescendingly colloquial language to pay the dues of the American Legion"

(364–65). The famous guest list in *The Great Gatsby,* moreover, includes a "Mr. P. Jewett, once head of the American Legion" (50–51). Further investigation into the membership status of both Gerlach and Fitzgerald appears difficult since contemporary membership records of the American Legion have not been preserved (Hovish).

48. Gerlach arrived back in New York City on January 4, 1911, on the *SS St. Paul* from Southampton. www.ellisislandrecords.org, Passenger Search, Frame #0645, line 5.

49. "Car Dealer Dying" 1–2. The report, along with a follow-up of the next day that reprints the 1930 photo of the "wealthy yachtsman" ("Would-Be Suicide Is Still Critical"), confirms that Gerlach "suffered financial reverses, among them the failure of an auto sales agency he started up at 150–10 Northern Boulevard, Flushing." The additional information that "the office of the German consulate in Manhattan said they had no record of a baron by the name of Gerlach" supports the conclusions arrived at in the present study about his origins. It is not at all unlikely that Gerlach, knowing about the role he had played in the composition of *The Great Gatsby,* had begun to style himself according to Gatsby's life and character.

50. Once more Fitzgerald may have borrowed a detail from the biography of his Great Neck friend Tommy Hitchcock. As Meyers notes, "After the war Tommy attended Harvard and (like Jay Gatsby) spent a term or two at Oxford" (103). A similarly intriguing source for this detail is suggested by Meredith, who points out that for the American Expeditionary Forces "there was an extensive program to send promising Americans to European educational institutions" (184) and cites a February 1919 AEF bulletin implementing the project (209 n3). As Meredith remarks, "These military facts are a history lesson today, but in Fitzgerald's time, they would have been current events and, therefore, relatively common knowledge, which loaned Gatsby's claims credibility" (184).

51. Gatsby's association with motorcars is put to good use throughout the novel, chiefly for the purposes of plot construction. In terms of theme, moreover, it serves Fitzgerald well to illustrate the opposition between old money and new money as much as between aristocrat and newcomer, the former sporting his time-honored equestrian culture that induces Tom Buchanan to boast that he is "the first man who ever made a stable out of a garage" (*GG* 92), the latter resorting to the incipient automotive culture of the early twenties, but easily put at a disadvantage when it comes to claiming social status. For a more detailed analysis of this aspect see chapter 2, "Dinner at the Buchanans': Beginning *The Great Gatsby.*"

52. In his unpublished biography of Cushman A. Rice, the late Dan Hardy is making a case for Rice as being the "forgotten farm type of Minnesota" referred

to in Fitzgerald's letter to Jamieson, as well as the actual model of Jay Gatsby. The facts about the long-term friendship between Rice and Gerlach emerged too late to have been considered in his study. No information was found by Hardy about any of Gerlach's activities in Cuba.

Chapter 2

1. Mary H. Rumsey, Letter to Willard Straight, February 22, 1911, The Dorothy Whitney Straight Elmhirst Papers, Division of Rare and Manuscript Collections, Cornell University Library.

2. An expanded version of this study was published in 1914 by Macmillan as *Feeblemindedness: Its Causes and Consequences* (see Kevles 325 n29), whereas the text as published in the bulletin was a reprint from *The American Breeders Magazine* of the previous year.

3. The close friendship between the Rumsey and the Hitchcock families continued after the death of Charles Cary Rumsey. Tommy Hitchcock was present when in 1925 Mary Harriman Rumsey visited Trujillo in Spain to select the site for her husband's statue of Francisco Pizarro, the conqueror of Peru, to be presented to the city ("Gives Pizarro Statue"). In 1929 the Hitchcocks moved to Sands Point on Manhasset Neck where they lived not far from Mary Rumsey (Aldrich 216).

4. Turnbull recounts two instances of Fitzgerald on horseback, each reflecting negatively on the author or his horsemanship (*Scott Fitzgerald* 88, 90).

5. Much like his friend Edmund Wilson in *The Crime in the Whistler Room*, Fitzgerald apparently was not at all bashful about using the names of real people or borrowing recognizable traits of character from friends, even for negative portrayals. The most obvious case is that of basing Tom Buchanan on Tommy Hitchcock. Another instance would seem to be the use of the name Sloane with its ready reference to the proprietors of W. & J. Sloane Furniture Company of New York. In 1923 there were two members of the well-connected family holding property in Sands Point on Manhasset Neck: Malcolm Douglas Sloane (1885–1924), a horseman certainly, although not a polo player (see "In the Berkshires"), owning the famous Lands End estate at Prospect Point. It is not at all unlikely, then, that the party on horseback visiting Gatsby's house is based entirely on actual members of the moneyed aristocracy of Long Island, the reactions to Gatsby reflecting the prevalent disdain of old money for new money.

6. "Book Talk: The Celt and the World," *Nassau Literary Magazine,* May 1917, rpt. in *F. Scott Fitzgerald: The Princeton Years* 120.

7. The same point had been made earlier by Jeffrey Louis Decker in "Gatsby's Pristine Dream: The Diminishment of the Self-Made Man in the Tribal Twenties" (1994).

8. "High scientific authority—geneticists, psychologists, anthropologists—drew upon expert 'evidence,' notably Henry Goddard's I.Q. tests of immigrants and Carl Brigham's analysis of the Army intelligence test results, to proclaim that a large proportion of immigrants bordered on or fell into the 'feebleminded' category and that their continued entrance into the country made, in Robert Yerkes's phrase, for the 'menace of race deterioration.' Whatever the symbolic meaning of the Statue of Liberty, American eugenicists like Charles Davenport stressed that the nation's future had to be taken into account. Davenport wrote to his brother William—a minister who was devoting his life to settlement-house work with Italian immigrants in Brooklyn, New York—'Just imagine what sort of country it will be . . . [in two hundred years] if the gates have, in the meantime, been wide open and population encouraged to come hither by the transportation companies and by the employers of the cheapest labor? . . . We don't want to make a State of Mississippi or worse out of New York City and Long Island'" (Kevles 94). Davenport's explicit mention of Long Island is interesting in terms of the genesis of *The Great Gatsby* as well as the world of the novel itself.

9. Ronald Berman also notes that "[p]art of Fitzgerald's experiment in this novel is the rendition of gesture that takes the place of speech" (*"The Great Gatsby" and Modern Times* 9–10).

Chapter 3

1. My translation of the text of *Immanuel Kant in seinen letzten Lebensjahren: Ein Beitrag zur Kenntnis seines Charakters und häuslichen Lebens aus dem täglichen Umgang mit ihm* of 1804 as reprinted in Hoffmann 301.

2. Fitzgerald's undergraduate record at Princeton indicates that he took Philosophy 301, a junior level course, in the 1916 fall term, obtaining a grade of A+, and went on to take Philosophy 302 in the 1917 spring term, in which he received a grade of A. There is further evidence of Fitzgerald's early as well as lasting interest in philosophy in the Princeton University Library collection of books owned by the author and also in the list of writers he drew up for Sheilah Graham's education in the College of One project. The collection includes Herbert Ernest Cushman's *A Beginner's History of Philosophy* (two volumes, 1911), the author's autographed copy

preserved from his college days, and Friedrich Paulsen's *Introduction to Philosophy* (2nd edition from the third German edition, 1895), once more an autographed copy, both works containing large sections on Kant. The list for Sheilah Graham includes the names of Voltaire, Descartes, Marx, and Spengler along with that of Kant. Moreover, under the heading of "How I Would Grade My Knowledge at 40," Fitzgerald gave himself the grade of B- for Philosophy, topped only by a B+ each for "Literature and Attendant Arts" and "History and Biography" (see Westbrook 280). I am obliged to James L. W. West III for furnishing the information about Fitzgerald's undergraduate record and examining the two items in the Princeton University Library.

3. Fitzgerald's claim is inaccurate since *The Decline of the West* was not available in English translation until 1926. For an explanation of the seeming disparity of dates see chapter 4, "Once by the Atlantic. . . ."

4. On page 254 Fitzgerald would have found what seems like a blueprint for certain scenes in *The Great Gatsby*. Actually, the author had previously mentioned these details to Wilson. In his play, "The Crime in the Whistler Room" (first performed in October 1924), Wilson has a character resembling Fitzgerald describe a gentleman bootlegger resembling Gatsby, and Fitzgerald noted in his copy of a 1937 reprint of the play in Wilson's *This Room and This Gin and These Sandwiches*, "I had told Bunny my plan for Gatsby" (75). See chapter 1, "Max von Gerlach, the Man behind Jay Gatsby."

5. The first to explore the affinity in plot and theme between the two novels was Robert Emmet Long in "*The Great Gatsby* and the Tradition of Joseph Conrad" of 1966.

6. Scholarly editions of *The Great Gatsby* all annotate the reference to Kant. While Bruccoli in the Cambridge University Press edition as well as in his *Apparatus for F. Scott Fitzgerald's "The Great Gatsby"* and Ruth Prigozy in the Oxford World's Classics edition are careful to point to the link between Kant's staring at the steeple and the activity of philosophical contemplation, James L. W. West III, in his edition of the author-marked galley proofs of the novel (*Trimalchio: An Early Version of "The Great Gatsby"*), goes on to suggest a general applicability of Kant's metaphysics to a reading of the text: "Kant's insistence that knowledge is limited to the world of phenomena, and that all attempts by man to know things-in-themselves (or noumena) will fail, is a theme of the novel and perhaps significant in this passage" (174). Another suggestion may be added as a complement to these notes. Given the significance of time in the passage that follows the Kant reference in *The Great Gatsby,* it is not impossible that Fitzgerald should have been aware of the position of time

in Kantian metaphysics. The discussion of time (along with that of space) played a prominent role in the philosopher's writings from his inaugural dissertation of 1770 to the *Critique of Pure Reason* of 1781 and 1787, notably in its section on *Aesthetik*. Time and space, to Kant, exist a priori; they are the two universal forms of perception into which all data of sense must be received. It is the prominence of time and space in the discussion of the essential conditions of sense perception, rather than Kant's reflections on time and space as pure notions, that could have encouraged the author of *The Great Gatsby* through the medium of his narrator's reflections to explore and to accentuate his own heightened awareness of time as an essential quality in his life as well as in his fiction.

Chapter 4

1. For the most detailed analysis of the influence of Adams on *The Beautiful and Damned,* see Moreland 121–25.

2. See also Lehan's earlier article, "Fitzgerald and Romantic Destiny" (1980), which specifies that the "*Century* was a magazine that Fitzgerald often read" (137). Dalton Gross, in "F. Scott Fitzgerald's 'The Great Gatsby' and Oswald Spengler's 'The Decline of the West'" (1970), suggests Henry de Man's "Germany's New Prophets" in the *Yale Review* 13:4, July 1924, pp. 665–83, as another plausible source of information on Spengler's ideas prior to the publication of the English translation of his work. Like Stewart, de Man points to Spengler's "rejection of the current theory of civilization as a continuous progressive process" (676), and he is quite specific in stressing the role of America: "Indeed, America furnishes Spengler with some of his most forceful arguments to prove that Occidental civilization has reached its final stages: the destruction of the 'land' by the 'city'; the replacement of 'organic' civilization by a purely 'mechanical,' intellectual, quantitative one; the decay of racial quality through the increasing sterility of the superior races; and the weakening of popular self-government by the increase of money-power" (677). A little later, he summarizes as follows: "[. . .] North America is to Europe in the development of Occidental civilization what Rome was to Greece in the ancient world: a late reflection which emphasizes the decay of the mother civilization through its artistic sterility, its matter-of-fact skepticism, its worship of material success and power, its incapacity for all new achievements, the old ones being merely repeated on a large scale" (680). But on the whole, the ten pages devoted to Spengler in de Man's survey are more abstract and less graphic than the ten pages of Stewart's article.

3. Ronald Berman justly describes the author as "a fluent translator of public ideas" ("Fitzgerald's Intellectual Context" 82) and provides what amounts to the most comprehensive and the most consistent study of Fitzgerald's work in its relation to both high culture and popular culture in *"The Great Gatsby" and Modern Times* (1994); *"The Great Gatsby" and Fitzgerald's World of Ideas* (1997); *Fitzgerald, Hemingway, and the Twenties* (2001); *Fitzgerald-Wilson-Hemingway: Language and Experience* (2003); *Modernity and Progress: Fitzgerald, Hemingway, Orwell* (2005); and *Translating Modernism: Fitzgerald and Hemingway* (2010).

Bibliography

Adams, Henry. *The Education of Henry Adams.* 1905. New York: The Modern Library, 1931.

Adams, James Truslow. *The Epic of America.* New York: Blue Ribbon Books, 1941.

Aldrich, Nelson W. Jr., *Tommy Hitchcock: An American Hero.* Privately printed (copyright Margaret Mellon Hitchcock), 1984.

"America Will Participate in the Kant Centenary." *New York Times* 21 Mar. 1924: 21.

Arnold, Matthew. "Dover Beach." 1867. *The New Oxford Book of English Verse, 1250–1950.* Chosen and ed. by Helen Gardner. Oxford: Oxford University Press, 1972. 703.

Bender, Bert. "'His Mind Aglow': The Biological Undercurrent in Fitzgerald's *Gatsby* and Other Works." *Journal of American Studies* 32.3 (Dec. 1998): 399–420.

Berliner Address-Buch für das Jahr 1874. Berlin: Druckschriften-Verlags-Comtoir, 1874. [also consulted: annual volumes for 1875, 1876, 1877]

Berliner Addressbuch 1914, Zweiter Band. Berlin: August Scherl, 1914.

Berman, Ronald. *Fitzgerald, Hemingway, and the Twenties.* Tuscaloosa: University of Alabama Press, 2001.

———. *Fitzgerald-Wilson-Hemingway: Language and Experience.* Tuscaloosa: University of Alabama Press, 2003.

———. "Fitzgerald's Intellectual Context." *A Historical Guide to F. Scott Fitzgerald.* Ed. Kirk Curnutt. Oxford: Oxford University Press, 2004. 69–84.

————. *"The Great Gatsby"and Fitzgerald'sWorld of Ideas.* Tuscaloosa: University of Alabama Press, 1997.

————. *"The Great Gatsby"and Modern Times.* Urbana: University of Illinois Press, 1994.

Black, Edwin. *The War Against the Weak: Eugenics and America's Campaign to Create a Master Race.* NewYork: FourWalls EightWindows, 2003.

"Blames Public for Laxness of Juries:Wayne B.Wheeler Says Miscarriage of Justice Is Not Due to Prohibition." *New York Times* 20 Feb. 1922: 10.

Bond, Harold L. *The Literary Art of Edward Gibbon.* Oxford: Oxford University Press, 1960.

Boyd, Ernest. *Portraits, Real and Imaginary.* NewYork: Doran, 1924.

Brennan, Joseph. American Protective League Report on Max Stork Gerlach for the American Intelligence. NewYork City, 1 Oct. 1918. Record Group 165. National Archives and Records Administration II, College Park, Maryland.

Bruccoli, Matthew J. *Apparatus for F. Scott Fitzgerald's "The Great Gatsby" [Under the Red,White, and Blue].* Columbia: University of South Carolina Press, 1974.

————. "'How Are You and the Family Old Sport?'—Gerlach and Gatsby." *Fitzgerald / Hemingway Annual 1975:* 33–36. Rpt. [with additions] Bruccoli, ed., *F. Scott Fitzgerald's "The Great Gatsby":A Documentary Volume* 20.

————. "Introduction." F. Scott Fitzgerald. *The Cruise of the Rolling Junk.* N. p. [1].

————. "Introduction." F. Scott Fitzgerald. *The Great Gatsby.* Ed. Matthew J. Bruccoli. Cambridge: Cambridge University Press, 1991. ix–lv.

————. *Some Sort of Epic Grandeur:The Life of F. Scott Fitzgerald.* NewYork: Harcourt Brace Jovanovich, 1981.

————. *Some Sort of Epic Grandeur:The Life of F. Scott Fitzgerald.* 2nd rev. ed. Columbia: University of South Carolina Press, 2002.

————, ed. *F. Scott Fitzgerald: Inscriptions.* Columbia: Bruccoli, 1988.

————, ed. *F. Scott Fitzgerald, Poems, 1911–1940.* Bloomfield Hills, Michigan, and Columbia, South Carolina: Bruccoli Clark, 1981.

————, ed. *F. Scott Fitzgerald's Ledger (A Facsimile).*Washington: Bruccoli Clark / NCR Microcard Books, 1973.

————, ed. *F. Scott Fitzgerald's "The Great Gatsby":A Documentary Volume.* Dictionary of Literary Biography 219. Detroit, Michigan: Bruccoli, 2000. (Cited parenthetically as *GG Documentary Volume*).

————, ed. *New Essays on "The Great Gatsby."* Cambridge: Cambridge University Press, 1985.

————, ed., with the assistance of Judith S. Baughman. *F. Scott Fitzgerald:A Life in Letters.* NewYork: Scribner's, 1994.

————, ed., with Judith S. Baughman. *F. Scott Fitzgerald on Authorship.* Columbia: University of South Carolina Press, 1996.

————, and Judith S. Baughman, eds. *Conversations with F. Scott Fitzgerald.* Jackson: University Press of Mississippi, 2004.

————, and Jackson R. Bryer, eds. *F. Scott Fitzgerald in His Own Time: A Miscellany.* Kent: Kent State University Press, 1971.

————, and Margaret Duggan, eds., with the assistance of Susan Walker. *Correspondence of F. Scott Fitzgerald.* New York: Random House, 1980.

Bryant, William Cullen. "The Prairies." 1833. *The New Oxford Book of American Verse.* Chosen and ed. by Richard Ellmann. New York: Oxford University Press, 1976. 35–37.

Bryce, Robert. "Without a Net." *Polo Magazine.* Oct. 1999. <http://www.thepolomagazine.com>.

Bury, J. B. "Introduction." Edward Gibbon. *The History of the Decline and Fall of the Roman Empire.* Ed. J. B. Bury. Vol. 1. London: Methuen, 1909. vii–xxiii.

"Calls on Friend, Attempts Suicide." *New York World Telegraph* 22 Dec. 1939.

Campbell, Persia. *Mary Williamson Harriman.* New York: Columbia University Press, 1960.

"Car Dealer Dying: Shot Himself in Head; Von Gerlach Tries Suicide in Village Apartment." *Long Island Star-Journal* 21 Dec. 1939: 1–2.

Card Index to Names of Persons in General Departmental Files, 1917–1930, and Box No. 151, PI-194 E-101 HM 1993. Record Group 60. General Records of the Department of Justice. National Archives and Records Administration II, College Park, Maryland.

Corso, Joseph. "One Not-Forgotten Summer Night: Sources for Fictional Symbols of American Character in *The Great Gatsby.*" *Fitzgerald / Hemingway Annual 1976:* 9–33.

Daniel, Anne Margaret. "'Blue as the Sky, Gentlemen': Fitzgerald's Princeton through *The Prince.*" *F. Scott Fitzgerald in the Twenty-first Century.* Ed. Jackson R. Bryer, Ruth Prigozy, and Milton R. Stern. Tuscaloosa: University of Alabama Press, 2003. 10–37.

de Man, Henry. "Germany's New Prophets." *Yale Review* 13.4 (July 1924): 665–83.

De Quincey, Thomas. "The Last Days of Immanuel Kant." 1827. *The Collected Writings of Thomas De Quincey—Vol. 4: Biographies and Biographic Sketches.* Ed. David Masson. Edinburgh: Black, 1890. 323–79.

Decker, Jeffrey Louis. "Gatsby's Pristine Dream: The Diminishment of the Self-Made Man in the Tribal Twenties." *Novel: A Forum on Fiction* 28 (Autumn 1994): 52–71.

Deffaa, Chip, ed. *F. Scott Fitzgerald: The Princeton Years: Selected Writings, 1914–1920.* Fort Bragg, California: Cypress House Press, 1996.

Dewey, John. "Kant After Two Hundred Years." *The New Republic* 30 Apr. 1924: 254–56.

Dilworth, Thomas. "*The Great Gatsby* and the Arrow Collar Man." *The F. Scott Fitzgerald Review* 7 (2009): 81–93.

Donaldson, Scott, ed. *Critical Essays on F. Scott Fitzgerald's "The Great Gatsby."* Boston: Hall, 1984.

Dreiser, Theodore. "My Brother Paul." *Twelve Men.* 76–109.

———. *Twelve Men.* New York: Boni and Liveright, 1919.

———. "W. L. S." *Twelve Men.* 344–60.

"Farm Sold at Auction to Diocese." *New York Times* 20 Jan. 1995: 5.

Fegley, Jonathan P. "'If I Couldn't Be Perfect I Wouldn't Be Anything': Teaching Becoming and Being in *The Great Gatsby.*" *Approaches to Teaching Fitzgerald's "The Great Gatsby."* Ed. Jackson R. Bryer and Nancy P. Van Arsdale. New York: Modern Language Association of America, 2009. 126–38.

Fitzgerald, F. Scott. "Absolution." 1924. *The Stories of F. Scott Fitzgerald.* 159–72.

———. *The Beautiful and Damned.* 1922. Ed. James L. W. West III. Cambridge: Cambridge University Press, 2008.

———. *The Cruise of the Rolling Junk.* 1924. Ed. with an introduction by Matthew J. Bruccoli. Bloomfield Hills, Michigan: Bruccoli Clark, 1976.

———. *F. Scott Fitzgerald on Authorship.* Ed. Matthew J. Bruccoli with Judith S. Baughman. Columbia: University of South Carolina Press, 1996.

———. *F. Scott Fitzgerald's Ledger: A Facsimile.* Ed. with an introduction by Matthew J. Bruccoli. Washington: Bruccoli Clark / NCR Microcard Editions, 1972.

———. *The Great Gatsby.* 1925. Ed. Matthew J. Bruccoli. Cambridge: Cambridge University Press, 1991. (Cited parenthetically as *GG*)

———. *The Great Gatsby.* Ed. Ruth Prigozy. Oxford: Oxford University Press, 1998.

———. *The Great Gatsby: A Facsimile of the Manuscript.* Ed. with an introduction by Matthew J. Bruccoli. Washington: Microcard, 1973. (Cited parenthetically as *MS*)

———. *The Great Gatsby: The Revised and Rewritten Galleys.* Introduced and arranged by Matthew J. Bruccoli. F. Scott Fitzgerald Manuscripts Vol. 3. New York: Garland, 1990. (Cited parenthetically as *RRG*)

———. *The Letters of F. Scott Fitzgerald.* Ed. Andrew Turnbull. New York: Scribner's, 1963.

———. "My Lost City." 1935/1940. *My Lost City.* 106–15.

———. *My Lost City: Personal Essays, 1920–1940.* Ed. James L. W. West III. Cambridge: Cambridge University Press, 2005.

———. *The Notebooks of F. Scott Fitzgerald*. Ed. Matthew J. Bruccoli. New York: Harcourt Brace Jovanovich / Bruccoli Clark, 1978.

———. "The Offshore Pirate." 1920. *Before Gatsby: The First Twenty-Six Stories*. Ed. Matthew J. Bruccoli with the assistance of Judith S. Baughman. Columbia: University of South Carolina Press, 2001. 262–91.

———. "Princeton." 1927. *My Lost City*. 6-15

———. *The Stories of F. Scott Fitzgerald: A Selection of 28 Stories*. Ed. with an introduction by Malcolm Cowley. New York: Scribner's, 1951.

———. "Ten Best Books I Have Read." *Jersey City Evening Journal* 24 Apr. 1923: 9. Rpt. Bruccoli, ed. *F. Scott Fitzgerald on Authorship*. 86.

———. "Three Cities." *Brentano's Book Chat* 1 (Sept.–Oct. 1921): 15, 28. Rpt. Bruccoli and Bryer, eds. *F. Scott Fitzgerald in His Own Time*. 124–26.

———. "'Three Soldiers': A Review by F. Scott Fitzgerald." *St. Paul Daily News*, 25 Sept. 1921, Feature Section, 6. Rpt. Bruccoli, ed. *F. Scott Fitzgerald on Authorship*. 48–50.

———. *Trimalchio: An Early Version of "The Great Gatsby."* Ed. James L. W. West III. Cambridge: Cambridge University Press, 2000.

———. *The Vegetable: Or, From President to Postman*. 1923. New York: Scribner's, 1976.

Fitzgerald, Zelda. *Save Me the Waltz*. 1932. Harmondsworth: Penguin, 1971.

———. ["'Show Mr. and Mrs. F. to Number—'"]. 1934. F. Scott Fitzgerald. *My Lost City*. 304–38.

Ford, Richard. "The Three Kings: Hemingway, Faulkner, and Fitzgerald." *Esquire* 100 (Dec. 1983): 577–86.

"George Y. Bauchle: Retired Lawyer Was a Graduate of Columbia—Dies at 60." *New York Times* 11 July 1939: 17.

Gerard, James W. Chapter 9, "The Americans at the Outbreak of Hostilities." *My Four Years in Germany*. New York: Doran, 1917. Web. 16 Aug. 2010. <http://net.lib.byu.edu/estu/wwi/memoir/Gerard/4yrs3.htm>.

Gerlach, Max A. Passport Application No. 01584, 4 Aug. 1914, to the American Embassy at Berlin. National Archives and Records Administration II, College Park, Maryland.

Gerlach, Max S. Draft Registration Card. *US World War II Draft Registration Cards, 1942*. Serial No. 4365, Max S. Gerlach, 26 Apr. 1942. National Archives and Records Administration II, College Park, Maryland.

———. Passport Application No. 140599, 15 Nov. 1919, to the Department of State at Washington, DC. National Archives and Records Administration II, College Park, Maryland.

Gerlach, Max Stork. Burial Records. 30 Oct. 1958. Folio 547. Frank E. Campbell, Inc., The Funeral Chapel, 1076 Madison Avenue, New York, New York 10028.

———. Index Card for Max S. Gerlach. Adjutant General's Office. Record Group 407. National Archives and Records Administration II, College Park, Maryland.

———. Ordnance Department Personalia Sheet #10408-1514. 6 Aug. 1918. Record Group 156. National Archives and Records Administration II, College Park, Maryland.

Gerlach, Max von. Calling Card. Enclosure in Belle Trenholm, Letter to Arthur Mizener, 10 June 1954. Arthur Mizener Papers (C0634). Box 1, Folder 18. Manuscripts Division, Department of Rare Books and Special Collections, Princeton University Library.

———. Letter to Arthur Mizener. 2 July 1951. Arthur Mizener Papers (C0634). Box 1, Folder 18. Manuscripts Division, Department of Rare Books and Special Collections, Princeton University Library.

———. Letter to Arthur Mizener. Undated [c. 1953–1954]. Arthur Mizener Papers (C0634). Box 1, Folder 18. Manuscripts Division, Department of Rare Books and Special Collections, Princeton University Library.

Gibbon, Edward. *The Autobiography of Edward Gibbon.* 1796. London: Dent, 1911.

———. *The History of the Decline and Fall of the Roman Empire.* 1776–1788. Ed. J. B. Bury. London: Methuen, 1909.

"Gives Pizarro Statue to City of Trujillo: Mrs. Mary Harriman Rumsey Visits Spain to Select Site for the Monument." *New York Times* 16 Apr. 1925: 10.

Goldstein, Judith S. *Inventing Great Neck: Jewish Identity and the American Dream.* New Brunswick, N.J.: Rutgers University Press, 2006.

Gross, Dalton. "F. Scott Fitzgerald's 'The Great Gatsby' and Oswald Spengler's 'The Decline of the West.'" *Notes and Queries* 17 (Dec. 1970): 467.

Grunewald, H. W. Report of 29 June 1917 to Bureau of Investigation, Department of Justice. In Re Max Gerlach, German Activities. Old German Files, 1909–1921. Case No. 8000-33016. Case Title: German Activities. Web. 5 Nov. 2008. <http://www.footnote.com/image/1003935>.

Haldane, Viscount. "Immanuel Kant, 1724–1924." *Literary Review* 19 Apr. 1924: 685–86.

Hall, Prescott F. "Immigration Restriction and World Eugenics." *Journal of Heredity* 10.3 (Mar. 1919): 125–27.

Hamburger Passagierlisten 1850–1934. 1931 – Band 390 (May 1931–June 1931), Blatt 48. Staatsarchiv Hamburg. <www.ancestry.com>.

Hamburg Passenger Lists. Handwritten Indexes, 1855–1934. 1925–1934 – Band 174 (1931 A–K). G. Staatsarchiv Hamburg. <www.ancestry.com>.

Hardy, Dan. "Cushman Rice: The Man Who Was Gatsby?" *Writing in the Margins.* St. Paul: University of St. Thomas Dept. of English, Spring 2008. 4–5.

———. "Kandiyohi County Adventurer Cushman Rice—The Image of Gatsby." Manuscript draft. 12 pp. 14 Sept. 2004. Copyright 2004 Daniel W. Hardy.

Hoffmann, Alfons, ed. *Immanuel Kant: Ein Lebensbild nach Darstellungen seiner Zeitgenossen Jachmann, Borowski, Wasianski.* Halle: Hugo Peter, 1902.

"Honor Kant in Konigsberg: 200 Academicians Mark 200th Birthday of Philosopher." *New York Times* 22 Apr. 1924: 4.

Hovish, Joe, Librarian and Curator, American Legion. Letter to the author. 22 Oct. 2001.

Howells, William Dean. *The Rise of Silas Lapham.* 1885. Ed. Don L. Cook. New York: Norton, 1982.

Hutchinson, Percy A. "Immanuel Kant: Author of a Profound Best-Seller." *New York Times Book Review* 20 Apr. 1924: 2.

"Immanuel Kant, 1724–1924." *The Nation.* 7 May 1924: 523–24.

"In the Berkshires: Fox Hunting Gives Rise to Picturesque Entertainments." *New York Times* 12 Sept. 1909: 6.

Index Card for Max Gerlach. Adjutant General's Office. Record Group 407. National Archives and Records Administration II, College Park, Maryland.

Index to Passports Issued Abroad 1906–1918. Microfilm M 1848. Roll 57. National Archives and Records Administration, Washington, DC.

Katcher, Leo. *The Big Bankroll: The Life and Times of Arnold Rothstein.* New Rochelle: Arlington House, 1958; New York: Harper, 1959.

Kehl, D. G. "Fitzgerald's 'Unbroken Series of Successful Gestures': From Gestural Tableau to Emotion and Idea." *The F. Scott Fitzgerald Review* 2 (2003): 116–33.

Kevles, Daniel J. *In the Name of Eugenics: Genetics and the Uses of Human Heredity.* Cambridge: Harvard University Press, 1995.

Klieger, P. Christiaan. *The Fleischmann Yeast Family.* Charleston: Arcadia Publishing, 2004.

Knowlin, Michael. *F. Scott Fitzgerald's Racial Angles and the Business of Literary Greatness.* New York: Palgrave Macmillan, 2007.

Kruse, Horst H. "The Real Jay Gatsby: Max von Gerlach, F. Scott Fitzgerald, and the Compositional History of *The Great Gatsby.*" *The F. Scott Fitzgerald Review* 1 (2002): 45–81.

Kuehl, John, ed. *The Apprentice Fiction of F. Scott Fitzgerald: 1907–1917.* New Brunswick: Rutgers University Press, 1965.

Lahrs, Friedrich. *Das Königsberger Schloß*. Stuttgart: Kohlhammer, 1956.

Lehan, Richard. *The City in Literature: An Intellectual and Cultural History*. Berkeley: University of California Press, 1998.

———. "Fitzgerald and Romantic Destiny." *Twentieth Century Literature* 26.2 (Summer 1980): 137–56.

———. "*The Great Gatsby* and Its Sources." Donaldson, ed. *Critical Essays on F. Scott Fitzgerald's "The Great Gatsby."* 66–74.

Lewis, Janet. "'The Cruise of the Rolling Junk': The Fictionalized Joys of Motoring." *Fitzgerald/Hemingway Annual 1978*: 68–81. Web. 25 Nov. 2009. <http://fitzgerald.narod.ru/critics-eng/lewis-rollingjunk.html>.

Long, Robert Emmet. "*The Great Gatsby* and the Tradition of Joseph Conrad: Part 1." *Texas Studies in Literature and Language* 8 (1966): 257–76.

MacKay, Robert B., Anthony Baker, and Carol Traynor, eds. *Long Island Country Houses and Their Architects 1860–1940*. New York: Norton, 1997.

Margolies, Alan. "The Maturing of F. Scott Fitzgerald." *Twentieth Century Literature* 43.1 (Spring 1997): 75–93.

"Max Gerlach, wealthy yachtsman. . . ." Unidentified Photo. *New York Evening Post* 18 Jan. 1930. Rpt. Bruccoli, ed. *F. Scott Fitzgerald's "The Great Gatsby": A Documentary Volume* 20.

Mencken, H. L. "Theodore Dreiser." *A Book of Prefaces*. 1916. Rpt. Alistair Cooke, ed. *The Vintage Mencken*. New York: Vintage, 1955. 35–56.

Meredith, James H. "Fitzgerald and War." *A Historical Guide to F. Scott Fitzgerald*. Ed. Kirk Curnutt. New York: Oxford University Press, 2004. 163–213.

Meyers, Jeffrey. *Scott Fitzgerald: A Biography*. New York: HarperCollins, 1994.

Millen, Gilmore. "Scott Fitzgerald Lays Success to Reading." *Los Angeles Evening Herald* 15 Jan. 1927. Clipping in F. Scott Fitzgerald's Scrapbook III: 131. F. Scott Fitzgerald Papers. Department of Rare Books and Special Collections, Princeton University Library. Rpt. Bruccoli and Baughman, eds. *Conversations with F. Scott Fitzgerald*. Jackson: University Press of Mississippi, 2004. 82–85.

Mizener, Arthur. *F. Scott Fitzgerald*. New York: Thames and Hudson, 1987.

———. *The Far Side of Paradise: A Biography of F. Scott Fitzgerald*. Boston: Houghton Mifflin, 1951.

———. *The Far Side of Paradise: A Biography of F. Scott Fitzgerald*. Rev. ed. Boston: Houghton Mifflin, 1965.

———. "Memories of Scott Fitzgerald." Letter to the Editor. *Times Literary Supplement*. 14 Nov. 1958: 65.

———. Letter to the Editor, *Times Literary Supplement* 5 Nov. 1958. Arthur Mizener Papers (C0634). Box 2, Folder 20. Manuscripts Division, Department of Rare Books and Special Collections, Princeton University Library.

———. Letter to Edmund Wilson. 22 Mar. 1948. Arthur Mizener Papers, Box 1, Folder 9. Special Collections, University of Delaware Library, Newark, Delaware.

———. Letter to Edmund Wilson. 12 Apr. 1948. Arthur Mizener Papers, Box 1, Folder 9. Special Collections, University of Delaware Library, Newark, Delaware.

———. Letter to Max von Guerlach. 15 Jan. 1951. Typescript copy. Arthur Mizener Papers (C0634). Box 1, Folder 18. Manuscripts Division, Department of Rare Books and Special Collections, Princeton University Library.

———. *Scott Fitzgerald and His World.* London: Thames and Hudson, 1972; New York: Putnam, 1972.

———. Undated TS note [c. 1951–1954]. Arthur Mizener Papers (C0634). Box 1, Folder 18. Manuscripts Division, Department of Rare Books and Special Collections, Princeton University Library.

Moreland, Kim. *The Medievalist Impulse in American Literature: Twain, Adams, Fitzgerald, and Hemingway.* Charlottesville: University Press of Virginia, 1996.

"Mrs. Rumsey Dies After Hunt Injury." *New York Times* 19 Dec. 1934: 1, 10.

Name Index to Correspondence of the Military Intelligence Division of the War Department General Staff 1917–1941. National Archives and Records Administration II, College Park, Maryland.

New York City Telephone Directory, 10 May 1922. New York: New York Telephone Company, American Telephone & Telegraph Co., 1922.

New York City Telephone Directory, 11 Oct. 1922. New York: New York Telephone Company, American Telephone & Telegraph Co., 1922.

New York City Telephone Directory, 13 Oct. 1926. New York: New York Telephone Company, American Telephone & Telegraph Co., 1926.

New York City Telephone Directory: Manhattan, New York City. New York: New York Telephone Company. Microfilm at New York Public Library, Reels 63 (Jan. 1950) to 71 (1957–1958).

New York Passenger Lists, 1820–1957. Max Gerlach. Web. 15 Feb. 2010. <http://search.ancestry.com>.

Ordnance Officers Called to Duty in World War I. Vol. 8. Record Group 156. National Archives and Records Administration II, College Park, Maryland.

"Pair Sit Reading Papers, Then He Shoots Himself." *New York Herald Tribune* 22 Dec. 1939.

Passenger List, Linea Aeropostal Venezolana. Arrival, Idlewild International Airport, New York, from Havana, Cuba, 26 Mar. 1950. Web. 13 Dec. 2006. <http://www.ancestry.com>.

Pershing, James Fletcher Jr., Draft Registration Card. *US World War I Draft Registration Cards, 1917–1918*. Serial No. 1439746, James Fletcher Pershing Jr., 5 June 1917. Web. 27 May 2013. <http://interactive.ancestry.com>.

"Pershing Quits Job as Aid to Dry Chief." *New York Times* 15 Aug. 1922: 13.

Pietrusza, David. *Rothstein: The Life, Times, and Murder of the Criminal Genius Who Fixed the 1919 World Series*. New York: Carroll and Graf, 2003.

Piper, Henry Dan. *F. Scott Fitzgerald: A Critical Portrait*. New York: Holt, Rinehart and Winston, 1965.

Piper, Roberta. "The Ghost in My House: A Reminiscence." *The F. Scott Fitzgerald Review* 5 (2006): 3–10.

———. Letter to *Princeton Alumni Weekly*. 14 Nov. 2002. Princeton Alumni Weekly: Letter Box. Web. 26 Apr. 2010. <http://www.princeton.edu/paw/web _exclusives/more/more_letters/>.

Rang- und Quartier-Liste der Königlich Preussischen Armee für 1883. Ed. Königliche Geheime Kriegs-Kanzlei. Berlin: Mittler, 1883. [also consulted: annual volumes for 1884 to 1889]

Real Estate Reference Map of Nassau County, Long Island. New York: E. Belcher Hyde Inc., 1923.

Richmond's Yonkers City Directory. New York: R. L. Polk & Co., 1902.

Riggio, Thomas P. "Dreiser, Fitzgerald, and the Question of Influence." *Theodore Dreiser and American Culture: New Readings*. Ed. Yoshinobo Hakutani. Newark: University of Delaware Press, 2000. 234–47.

Rumsey, Mary H. Letter to Willard Straight. 22 Feb. 1911. The Dorothy Whitney Straight Elmhirst Papers. Division of Rare and Manuscript Collections, Cornell University Library.

Salpeter, Harry. "Fitzgerald, Spenglerian," *New York World*, 3 Apr. 1927. Rpt. as "The Next Fifteen Years Will Show How Much Resistance There Is in the American Race." Bruccoli and Bryer, eds. *F. Scott Fitzgerald in His Own Time*. 274–77.

Scribner, Charles III. "Introduction." F. Scott Fitzgerald. *The Vegetable: Or, From President to Postman*. New York: Scribner's, 1976. v–xx.

Ship Manifest of *SS Devonian*. Arrival, Boston Harbor, from Liverpool, England, 10 Oct. 1914. Boston Passenger Lists 1891–1943. Microfilm Roll #229. Web. 10 Feb. 2005. <http://search.ancestry.com>.

Ship Manifest of *SS Esperanza*. Arrival, New York Harbor, from Havana, Cuba, 7 Apr. 1924. Web. 12 June 2001. <http://www.ellisisland.org/>.

Ship Manifest of *SS Furnessia*. Arrival, New York Harbor, from Glasgow, Scotland, 30 Nov. 1894. Web. 8 Feb. 2005. <http://www.ellisisland.org/>.

Ship Manifest of *SS Hamburg*. Arrival, New York Harbor, from Hamburg, Germany, 15 May 1931. Web. 15 Feb. 2010. <http://search.ancestry.com>.

Ship Manifest of *SS Havana*. Arrival, New York Harbor, from Havana, Cuba, 24 July 1912. Web. 6 Dec. 2001. <http://www.ellisisland.org/>.

Ship Manifest of *SS Morro Castle*. Arrival, New York Harbor, from Havana, Cuba, 9 Mar. 1920. Web. 9 Oct. 2010. <http://www.ellisisland.org>.

Ship Manifest of *SS Saratoga*. Arrival, New York Harbor, from Havana, Cuba, 2 Mar. 1909. Web. 31 Mar. 2004. <http://www.ellisisland.org/>.

Ship Manifest of *SS Saratoga*. Arrival, New York Harbor, from Havana, Cuba, 21 Feb. 1911. Web. 4 Feb. 2005. <http://www.ellisisland.org/>.

Ship Manifest of *SS St. Paul*. Arrival, New York Harbor, from Southampton, England, 4 Jan. 1911. Web. 6 Dec. 2001. <http://www.ellisisland.org/>.

Ship Manifest of *SS Vigilancia*. Arrival, New York Harbor, from Veracruz, Mexico, 6 Sept. 1903. Web. 4 Feb. 2005. <http://www.ellisisland.org/>.

Slater, Peter Gregg. "Ethnicity in *The Great Gatsby*." *Twentieth Century Literature* 19.1 (Jan. 1973): 53–63.

Solomon, Barbara Probst. "Westport Wildlife." *The New Yorker* 9 Sept. 1996: 78–85.

Spinzia, Raymond E. and Judith A. *Long Island's Prominent North Shore Families: Their Estates and Their Country Homes*. College Station, TX: VirtualBookworm, 2006.

Stewart, W. K. "The Decline of Western Culture: Oswald Spengler's 'Downfall of Western Civilization' Explained." *Century Magazine* 108.5 (Sept. 1924): 589–98.

"Stinnes Honored Kant: Late Industrialist Paid for Monument on Philosopher's Grave." *New York Times* 24 Apr. 1924: 32.

Stork, Max [a.k.a. Max Stork Gerlach]. Photo [1915]. New York City Municipal Archives Online Gallery: PDE: Police Department Evidence: pde_0368.

Strohl, Daniel. "Bootleggers, Used Car Dealers and *The Great Gatsby* — On the Trail of Max Gerlach." *Hemmings Blog*. Hemmings Daily, 18 Feb. 2010. Web. 19 Feb. 2010. <http://blog.hemmings.com/index.php/2010/02/18/bootleggers -used-car-dealers-and-the-great-gatsby-on-the-trail-of-max-gerlach/>.

Trenholm, Belle. Letter to Arthur Mizener. 10 June 1954. Arthur Mizener Papers (C0634). Box 1, Folder 18. Manuscripts Division, Department of Rare Books and Special Collections, Princeton University Library.

Trow's General Directory of the Boroughs of Manhattan and Bronx, City of New York, for the Year 1910. New York: Trow, 1910.

Turnbull, Andrew. *Scott Fitzgerald.* New York: Charles Scribner's Sons, 1962.

Turner's Annual Directory of Yonkers. Yonkers, N.Y.: W. L. Richmond, 1903. [also consulted: annual volume for 1904]

1900 United States Federal Census. Twelfth Census of the United States: 1900 [database online]. State New York. County Westchester. Yonkers. Supervisor's District No. 3. Enumeration District No. 132. Sheets No. 8 and 9. 5 June 1900 (as of 1 June).

1910 United States Federal Census. Thirteenth Census of the United States: 1910 [database online]. State New York. County New York. Manhattan Borough. Ward 19. Supervisor's District No. 1. Enumeration District No. 1063. Sheet No. 10 A. 21 Apr. 1910 (as of 15 Apr.).

1920 United States Federal Census. Fourteenth Census of the United States: 1920 [database online]. State New Jersey. County Middlesex. Raritan Township. Supervisor's District No. 3. Enumeration District No. 59. Sheet No. 30. 23 Feb. 1920 (as of 1 Jan.).

1940 United States Federal Census. Sixteenth Census of the United States: 1940 [database online]. State New York. County New York. Manhattan Borough. Supervisor's District No. 16. Enumeration District No. 31-1049. Sheet No. 4 A. 5 Apr. 1940 (as of 1 Apr.).

United States v. Max Gerlach. Court Docket C 48-225 (S.D.N.Y. 5 Aug. 1927). National Archives and Records Administration, Northeast Region, New York City.

United States v. Max V. Gerlach. Court Docket C 46-768 (S.D.N.Y. 9 May 1927). National Archives and Records Administration, Northeast Region, New York City.

Walbridge, Earle. *Literary Characters Drawn from Life.* New York: Wilson, 1936.

Wasianski, Ehregott Andreas Christoph. *Immanuel Kant in seinen letzten Lebensjahren: Ein Beitrag zur Kenntnis seines Charakters und häuslichen Lebens aus dem alltäglichen Umgang mit ihm.* 1804. *Immanuel Kant: Ein Lebensbild nach Darstellungen seiner Zeitgenossen Jachmann, Borowski, Wasianski.* Ed. Alfons Hoffmann. Halle: Hugo Peter, 1902. 288–432.

West, James L. W., III. *The Perfect Hour: The Romance of F. Scott Fitzgerald and Ginevra King, His First Love.* New York: Random House, 2005.

Westbrook, Robert. *Intimate Lies: F. Scott Fitzgerald and Sheilah Graham: Her Son's Story.* New York: Harper Collins, 1995.

Wharton, Edith. *The Age of Innocence*. 1920. Harmondsworth: Penguin, 1974.

Wilson, B. F. "Notes on Personalities: F. Scott Fitzgerald." *The Smart Set* Apr. 1924. Rpt. Bruccoli and Bryer, eds. *F. Scott Fitzgerald In His Own Time*. 414–20.

Wilson, Edmund. "Imaginary Conversations: II. Mr. Van Wyck Brooks and Mr. Scott Fitzgerald." *The New Republic* 30 Apr. 1924: 249–54. Rpt. in slightly edited versions as "Imaginary Dialogues: II. The Delegate from Great Neck: Mr. Van Wyck Brooks and Mr. Scott Fitzgerald" in Edmund Wilson, *Discordant Encounters* (1926), and as "Imaginary Dialogues: II. The Delegate from Great Neck: Mr. F. Scott Fitzgerald and Mr. Van Wyck Brooks" in Edmund Wilson, *The Shores of Light: A Literary Chronicle of the Twenties and Thirties* (1952).

———. Letter to Arthur Mizener. 30 Mar. 1948. Arthur Mizener Papers, Box 1, Folder 9. Special Collections, University of Delaware Library, Newark, Delaware.

———. Letter to Arthur Mizener. 22 Feb. 1950. Arthur Mizener Papers, Box 1, Folder 10. Special Collections, University of Delaware Library, Newark, Delaware.

———. *This Room and This Gin and These Sandwiches*. New York: New Republic, 1937.

Wittke, Carl. *German-Americans and the World War*. Columbus, Ohio: The Ohio State Archaeological and Historical Society, 1936.

"Would-Be Suicide Is Still Critical: Von Gerlach's Condition Shows No Change." *Long Island Star-Journal* 23 Dec. 1939: 1.

Index